The tomorrow thinker

By

Magandazi.D. Katakaya

I0466324

INTRODUCTION

A ton of questions might run through your mind right now. Questions like "Why do I need to compare myself to others? How is he more successful than I am? Why am I not as lucky?"

If you are wondering; it can be out of jealousy, greed, desire, or more. It might be easy to say, but you should not envy anyone. The only person you should try to be envious of and be better than, is the person you were yesterday. If you can do this, then you become better with each day that passes.

And yes, it would be a lie if I told you that the road to being greater is easy as you try to live better each day. The truth is that it won't be easy at all. Each day is filled with its barriers and challenges, but it is also full of many different opportunities.

As you try to be better than whom you were yesterday, you will begin to realize, appreciate and enjoy the gifts and benefits life has in store for you. And you may even start to discover various possibilities in each given challenge. So, be better than who you were yesterday, even if it happens only via one percent each day, week or month.

What I mean is that even if you make mistakes, it is your ability not to allow your errors to influence or control you. It is what makes you who you are. And if there is one thing I learned time and time again is to be better than whom I was yesterday.

Therefore, if you do not do something right or you know you made a blunder for one reason or the other, do not give those mistakes power. I know that we are all going through this. So, do not let the errors you make rule your life, learn from them, move on and do not judge you or what you can do.

Believe it or not, the power you acquired through all of your experiences can help you avoid many costly mistakes. You just have to learn, work, live and strive to be better than the person you were yesterday. I am not telling you to try to reach perfection but only that you do not have to live your life in the same way if you are unsatisfied with it.

After all, you have the power to make any change your heart desires. If you do not believe you are capable of it, just imagine for an instant, that one day you are doing better. Would not that make you feel like some renewed confidence is soaring through you? And is not that a better use of your time than some negative feelings? By thinking that way, you will move forward and grow to be a remarkable person.

TABLE OF CONTENT

CHAPTER ONE

Understanding your current situation for better future

Do you have that disappointing feeling of continuously making the very same mistakes? Are you simply tired of the downfalls in your current life and you feel as though you only experience the harsh side of life full of annoying limitations? Well, if you are adamantly looking for explanations to the downfalls and limitations in your current life, then a past life reading may provide some answers. The theory of reincarnation is real and supported by the unexplained. This includes children born speaking certain foreign languages outside of their heritage and a plethora of esoteric phenomena and ancient belief systems support reincarnation. Better still, this theory is endorsed by individuals who have died and revived as well people who have experienced outer-body experiences or astral projection. Many of these individuals can attest to both past and present life incarnations prior to regaining full consciousness.

Often at times, the downfalls and limitations in our lives are highly connected to past life experiences. Having a past life regression reading can reveal some reason behind adversity or good fortune. Obtaining such knowledge enables you to eliminate or comprehend matters you're currently struggling with. Often the obtainment of such a reading is a professional procedure, where a gifted individual is able to see past your current life into the experiences of your previous life. These readings are unmediated revelations that are revealed through hypnosis, astral connection to higher planes or often with the professional help of a regression therapist. However, this regression process can become difficult and even impossible for those individuals who have exceedingly strong egos and cannot be hypnotized.

The experiences and lessons of past lives are responsible for making us who we are today by evolving the higher self. By identifying and focusing on particular events one may begin to understand the mysteries in our current situations, perceptions and experiences. Certainly, everyone has distinct questions that they feel influences their current lives and can relate intuitively to familiarity yet are challenged by the specifics.

For instance, some ⬚uestions which concern experience of a past life are instrumental in explaining feelings such as seemingly unfounded fears, obsessions, sadness, reoccurring patterns and even depressions experienced in current lives. An experienced reader may be able to retrieve information prior to reincarnation--pinpointing the exact experience that brings about the above undesirable feeling and chooses the right channel from which to heal, recover, or comprehend current issues.

Once you are able to understand the relationship between past and present life cycles, then you are enabled to make dramatic changes in your current life by newfound enlightenment and understanding.

Our character in the current life represents a culmination of distinct past life experiences. These experiences and memories affect our behaviour in many aspects. Past life readings can assist in knowledge and knowledge can provide healing of psychological and emotional trauma resulting from a past life, giving an individual the chance to let go and bring a beneficial change which also includes accomplishing karmic challenges and further evolution of the higher self. Past life regression will also help you comprehend and understand your true character, enabling you to draw positive interest in some specifics, be it a talent or endeavours.

How to Change Your Current Circumstances And Get The Results You Want

What can you do to become more aware, work at your full potential, and realize your goals? What will allow you to choose positive thoughts even in gloomy situations? It is your level of awareness.

There are seven levels of awareness listed here from the lowest to the highest level:

1. Animal

2. Mass

3. Aspiration

4. Individual

5. Discipline

6. Experience

7. Mastery

All of us primarily function at one of these levels. According to where we are in our lives at any given time, we may bounce back and forth between levels. We should strive to reach the highest level of mastery where we are in full control and getting the best results in life. Keep in mind that you could be operating on several levels depending on the particular area of your life. You may have ascended in development more so in one area of life than the other.

Level 1: Animal

This level of awareness is the stimulus-response level, also known as the reactionary or the fight, flight or freeze level. There is very little, if any, though at this level. This is the level a person is at when they allow what's going on in their current circumstances and/or reality dictates how they react. To react or respond is a choice. Reacting is a negative choice and responding is a positive one. Reacting implies that we have given control of our lives (our circumstances) to someone or something else.

We surrender to other people or things. At this level, we do not anticipate that which is to come because we are too busy putting out the fire before us, so we are unaware of new fires developing. Many give themselves to alcohol, drugs, or other negative external forces to control their circumstances, temporarily of course and only in appearance, when the real problem, of course, is still there and, in most cases, compounded to a larger scale because of ignoring it and because of adding another negative to it.

Responding to a situation is a positive choice. It is proactive and anticipates those things to come. Responding is preceded by thought. In responding, we take charge and have command over how the situation affects us. We also have control over how it affects us internally.

Level 2: Mass

At this level, an individual is concerned more about what others think about them. And it's not what others actually "think." It is what they think others think. Comments like "what will my best friend think," "what will my boss think" are common questions asked at this level. This is the conforming level of awareness or the "following the crowd" level. It is where the majority of people live their lives. Conformity. Not really thinking. Similar to the sheep mentality of simply following the leader, no questions asked. This level resembles going along with the current popular viewpoints. There is the minimal independent thought going on at this level. This person does not consciously choose the things that they want. They ask others what they think they should do with their life, problems, money, job, etc.

If you must follow others, follow the one or two folks who are doing things differently than the masses. It is a good chance that they have put some thought into what they are doing. Most people do not think. George Bernard Shaw said that 2 per cent of people think; 3 per cent of people think that they are thinking and 95 per cent of people would rather die than think! It is not a coincidence that 1 per cent of the world's population earns 96 per cent of the money being made. Break out of the "mass" level of consciousness and claim the life of your dream, the life you were created for.

Successful people do not follow the masses. They are independent thinkers. If you wish to achieve success, realize that it is not an easy path to follow. You will face ridicule from strangers, family, and friends. Remember that your first responsibility is to be true to yourself and do whatever fulfils you and makes you happy. Bob Proctor states, "The masses are obsessed with conformity rather than creativity."

Level 3: Aspiration

This is where you desire to be, do, or have more than your current circumstances. Unfortunately, it is desire without action. One could say this is the area where there is a lot of wishful thinking going on. No real change occurs here. As a person starts to read quality information or listen to others with quality information - like Wallace D. Wattles, Zig Ziglar, Bob Proctor, Napoleon Hill, Bob Burg, Paul Martinelli, and others - that person starts to realize that there is something more than they're capable of. This is the level where you are beginning to wake up. You now want to break away from the masses and become an individual. You know that there is something more than you are capable of.

Many people become stuck at this level because their new desires are just wishes until they back them with action. You may desire to earn more money. Desire is derived from the Latin word da-sire, which means "to give birth to." Wallace D. Wattles says, "The desire for riches is simply the capacity for larger life seeking fulfilment; every desire is the effort of an unexpressed possibility to come into action. It is power seeking to manifest which causes desire. That which makes you want more money is the same as that which makes the plant grow; it is Life, seeking fuller expression."

A person earning $50,000 per year is not earning that because they want to. They desire to earn far more than that. However, when this person is presented with the idea of earning $200,000 per year, he will reject the idea. Now, why would he reject the idea? Because that idea is far beyond what he is currently getting in his life. He thinks that he cannot earn more.

Decide to believe in yourself. Take charge of your own self-concept and beliefs. With enough positive self-talk and positive visualization combined with the proper training, coaching, and practice, anyone can learn to do almost anything. You must choose to believe that you can do anything you set your mind to. You can-it is a fact.

Level 4: Individual

After aspiring something bigger and better than your current circumstances, you begin to acknowledge that you are a worthwhile, amazing individual that is capable of amazing things. But this level, by itself, won't cut it. The individual level is unquestionably and totally dependent on the fifth level. This is when you begin to express your uniqueness as a human being. You take action. You become aware that there never has been, or will be, another expression of life like you.

Here, you begin to express your uniqueness through your actions. You are out of your head and into your uniqueness. You realize that there is no one like you. Only you possess your special gifts and talents. You move into action because you have the faith to move toward your desires.

If we can think it, we can do it. Keep your mind only on the things you desire. If you focus on what you want rather than what you do not want, you will know when it is time to move into action. Your actions will be effortless. Doors will open, and the entire universes will conspire to assist you with your desire.

You begin to dream. Once you step into the action, everything that you are seeking is also seeking you. You begin to live on purpose instead of by chance. Your goals begin to manifest.

You leave your comfort zone because you realize that this is necessary for change to take place. All growth takes places outside the comfort zone.

Abraham Maslo said that either we advance forward in the direction of our dreams or we revert backwards into safety.

Level 5: Discipline

This level is absolutely critical to the person who has aspired to break away from the mass level of awareness. Here discipline is required. By discipline, I mean the ability to give ourselves a command and follow through on it regardless of what is happening. This means to stay on course regardless of what the masses are doing and/or saying. Without disciplining oneself to take action, there will be insufficient force to make that break from the mass.

Are you willing to devote yourself to do anything necessary to make the goals and dreams you have become a reality? Are you able to become disciplined enough to see that what you must do to make your desires manifest is to be totally focused on the result from the beginning of any task?

Are you willing to work through any challenge or obstacle and turn it into an opportunity for growth and transformation as you build your business and character?

When you are devoted to being disciplined in all areas of your life, amazing things will happen. Being disciplined is a way of being that allows for abundant thinking so that when a limited belief pops up, you can see it for what it is and move through it with a conviction and determination that will bring you closer and closer to the results you want in any area of your life. Be disciplined about who you are and watch as the floodgates of infinite opportunity shower you with unlimited success.

Level 6: Experience

At this level, you recognize that all the answers or how's that you are looking for are really found from within. As you look within yourself, the spirit brings to you the ideas and people you require to accomplish the task at hand. As the individual applies discipline and does the things that will elevate one to new levels, the experience gained will reinforce that person's awareness of his or her own abilities. The difference between learning and experience is the discovery that the answers are within. "That which we persist in doing becomes easier to do. Not that the nature of the thing has changed, but that our ability to do has increased."

As you look within yourself, God brings to you the ideas and people you require to accomplish your desires. We have a wonderful world of power, possibility, and promise that is within us. Because within us is the mind and the mind is the creative cause of all that transpires in the experience and our lives. We can learn to use our mind constructively, and we can learn to correctly use these hidden powers, forces, and faculties.

When you apply steadfast discipline and do the things that will elevate you to new levels, the experience gained reinforces your awareness of your amazing abilities. This, in turn, leads to great accomplishments.

When you see the desired results manifest, you will become stronger in how you practice and do more of the same. When you do not see the desired results, you will make the necessary corrections and then practice with discipline until that desire manifests.

Level 7: Mastery

At this level of awareness, there is a higher level of thought. This is where a person will truly begin to respond instead of reacting. A person will stop and think, think and act. At this level of awareness, there is a higher level of humour, creativity, enthusiasm, excitement, love, and gratitude. We have developed the mindset needed to function from an abundant perspective.

We are no longer controlled by habitual patterns that our paradigms have created. Our minds are very calm. We know that whatever the challenge, adversity, or question we need an answer to, we will receive it. It is in the silence and calmness that we hear the answers. This is a very different way to live especially in these challenging times.

Mastery is the highest level that we can attain. Only a small percentage of the population reaches this point; however, we all have the mental faculties and capacity to do so. The feedback that we receive at the sixth level, experience, allows us to master what we want to accomplish in our life. These individuals have learned the laws of the universe. They understand how the science and process operates, and they have fine-tuned their methods based upon their experience. They are quite effective at attracting success, wealth, and resources. They are goal achievers.

Life just seems to flow here. One has reached a higher level of thought. This person truly thinks and takes the action that moves them in the direction of what is desired. Here, you become the captain of your own ship.

It takes a while to achieve this awareness level. It takes persistence and discipline. Since we only have one life to live, why not strive to make it a masterpiece?

"No man is free who is not a master of himself", **Epictetus**

Ways to Feel Better About Your Current Situation

Your current situation does not have to dictate the way you feel. Complaining and feeling depressed about it is a habit we've learnt and practised over the years. It's time to create a new habit so you can begin to feel better about your current situation and become proactive in its resolution.

If your current situation has you feeling depressed, instead of absorbing more of that negative energy, why not try these 3 ways so you can begin to feel better.

- **Know That This Is Only Temporary**

Although your current situation may feel like it's taking forever to resolve, know that this is only temporary. Just as the sun always comes out after every storm, so too, your adversities will subside. Don't recreate any more turbulence by focusing on how terrible it is right now. For what you focus on will only magnify in your mind's eye and what you focus your attention on will draw you into that experience.

Stop and ask, "Are the thoughts I'm focused on taking me in the direction of a brighter day, toward resolution? Or are they leading me into a cycle of experiences I don't want?"

- **Look For The Hidden Gems**

Opportunities sometimes come to us cloaked in the form of adversity. Look for the hidden gems in your situation. For example, if you got laid off of your job, what opportunities are waiting for you?

You may think that it may be another job right away but perhaps in the grand scope of things, this may be a time for you to deepen your spiritual connection, something that you could not do with your previous job.

And as you take the time to reconnect with the Great Universal Spirit, doors begin to open for you which would not have happened had you not taken the time to clear out the mental and emotion debris in your life.

- **Become Proactive To Find A Solution**

Instead of whining about how bad things have become focus on the solution. You see, you may be thinking that you've been doing all the physical things to bring resolution to your current situation and you may be right. But if you're focused on how things are not working out for you, you're sabotaging your own progress and blocking your success from coming to you.

You must become mentally and emotionally proactive as well - focusing on the solution and expecting that all will work out on your behalf. Feel it and see it happening for you. And out of that inner confidence go forward and do what can do and as you go on your way pay attention to the doors that are opening for you.

Ways To View Your Life As Optimistic, Regardless Of Your Current Situation.

Many people may look at their current situation instead of where he or she desires to be. They focus on what their life looks like today, instead of what he or she would like for it to look like in the future. No matter where you are at in your life, you can still feel optimistic about where you are going.

Below are 3 ways to feel optimistic about your life, regardless of your current situation:

1. Look At Your Life From An Optimistic Viewpoint:

Your current situation does not have to determine your destination. And by that I mean, that where you are at does not have to be the end of it. You can be more, do more and have more. There can be a great life ahead of you, and if you want it then you can have it.

When you begin to look at your life from an optimistic viewpoint, it gives you hope for the future. If we continue to only focus on our current situation, then it is not likely that we will be motivated to do things, that will help us achieve the life we deserve to live. So no matter how your life is now, it can get better, so be optimistic.

2. Find Things To Be Thankful For:

Finding something in your life to be thankful for can make you feel fulfilled, even in your current situation. Yes, it may be a fact that you are going through a lot, and things may not seem to be working in your best interest. But if you can just find one thing in your life to be thankful for, that can help you look at your situation from a brighter perspective.

Many people say "I don't have anything to be thankful for." But we all have something to be thankful for, even if it is just the fact that we have been blessed to see another day. Once you find one thing to be thankful for, then keep thinking of more things. You can even make yourself a "Things I am thankful for list," and carry it with you. You can refer to your list whenever you need inspiration, or to feel better about where you are it in life.

3. Speak What You Want, And Not What You Don't Want:

To feel better about your life, as it is currently, you must speak words of success and not failure. Regardless of where you are at in life, if you only use degrading and negative words about your situation, that is not going to help you feel better. Matter of fact, it will more than likely make you feel worse.

You should only speak words of life, into your life. Never refer to your life as a failure, hopeless or pathetic. Even if that is how you feel, don't say it. Speak words that are going to help you look at your life in a positive light, and that can help you become inspired, and motivated to work on improving your life.

Seeing your life differently may not happen overnight. But just keep saying what you want your life to look like, have faith, and take action. If you are dedicated and committed, eventually you will see results.

A Prayer to Come Out of Your Current Situation to a More Positive & Empowering One.

There are moments of despair or crisis we have to get along everyday life. What I give in this section is a wonderful magical prayer that will work almost every time to come out of your situation to land in a more positive one.

This prayer can be said at any time of the day and can be shortened or expanded as you like. It concentrates mainly on gratitude as it will work wonderfully with the Universe to pay you better times. There are, however, other aspects as well, for example, what you desire from God fervently and how to say it to get it. It covers aspects such as, why you are a believer of God and let Him know it and also how to ask for forgiveness from God for making mistakes if any while saying your prayer.

Here goes:

Thank you Almighty God for all blessings. Advanced thanks for those blessings that are already on the way to come to me.

The way you have kept your grace over me, I hope and pray that you will continue to do so and protect me.

I am a believer of You because I consider you, God, the Almightiest, the most Gracious and the most Merciful. As a believer of God, my prime desire is to ask You to cease to give me hard hardships, punishments, lessons or disappointments. My biggest desire is to ask for the things that I have already asked You about.

I ask for abundance and prosperity.

I ask for good health of my family and me as well as friends and well-wishers.

I ask for wellness & safety of all concerned.

I lay my problems in your hands. Please solve them for me. You can fix anything.

I trust in You, belief in You, have faith in You and rely on You. I trust in myself, belief in myself, have faith in myself and rely on myself.

Always give me the right guidance and show me the right way.

Thank you God for all blessings, I repeat.

If I have erred somewhere in saying this prayer, I ask for your forgiveness.

Please cease to give me shortcomings or the severe tests on me.

I hope everyone softens towards me.

I hope I can proceed towards my desired destination.

Thank you for all the blessings, I repeat.

This is the magic wonderful prayer that will work wonders. Say it as often as you like and you will benefit.

It really is simple but it covers everything you would like to change your situation to a more improved one.

This prayer is good on the overall in that it flip-flops your thoughts to more positive ones and therefore your situation also changes accordingly.

Simple Ways to Change The Way You Look On Your Troubling Situation

The way you look at your troubling situation could either entrap you or create the way out for you. Most people tend to look at their situation and worry about how they're going to get out of it. Worry is not creative thinking even though often times we think it's doing us some good or showing that we care.

Your mental and emotional energies transmit to the universal power what you desire to experience in your life. And if you are sending off the energy of fear and hopelessness through your thoughts and emotions that's what you will continue to create in your life. As a matter of fact, worry blinds you from seeing any possible way out of your current condition.

1. Elevate Your Thoughts

Every thought has a frequency and attracts similar thoughts to it until it takes on shape and form. Positive thoughts are more powerful than negative thoughts. So as you observe your own thoughts, are they positive high-frequency thoughts or are they negative low-frequency thoughts? Choose carefully.

2. Shift Your Perspective

How can you look at your situation differently? Instead of focusing on how bad things are, can you find something that's positive? Look for it.

Instead of focusing on how your pay cheque has reduced, be thankful that you do have a paychque, to begin with, in the first place. You may ask "How can I even be thankful for this paycheque when it could hardly pay the bills?"

By being thankful for what you have now puts you in a positive energy vibration that will attract to you more similar energy to it. You're opening the door for miracles to happen for you either you'll find things on sale, your pay increases or you find inspired ideas to help you better manage what you already have.

3. Free Your Mind

Release the negative energy of worry and hopelessness and free your mind from mental debris. Let go of your care knowing that all is working out for your good. Ask, "What do I want this outcome to be? How can I resolve this situation? What else can I do?"

These are positive questions that put you in the flow of creative energy to bring change to your current situation. What answers come back to you? Though simple and subtle they may be, follow through with them and start with what you can right now.

CHAPTER TWO

Importance of planning and strategizing for a better future

Many of us live from day to day without looking ahead to what we truly want or proper planning if we do, it's just a dream that may or may not come true. Life Coaching can help you turn that dream to reality, to set goals and targets in small manageable steps. It's easy to drift on in life, wishing you had taken a different path, hoping it will get better, personally and financially. After all, it can be a comfort to stay with what you know. A life coach can help you to remove fears that stop you, change limiting beliefs to empowering ones and help you to control your thoughts. Many people are afraid of failing, but what if you believed there was no such thing as failure, only the results of an action? If something you do doesn't work, do it differently next time. What if you truly believed that to never try was a failure - would that not free you up to go ahead and have a go? How can you know what you are capable of unless you give yourself a chance? By uncovering limiting beliefs, for example, "life is a struggle", and changing them to something more empowering such as "life is for living", it can change your whole outlook on life.

Any kind of plan is probably better than no plan at all. But do you know the reason so many plans fail or succeed only as a faded, watered-down version of what they're supposed to be? It could be inadeuate information gathering, or a lacklustre vision or poor implementation or non-existent management. All of these things will come into play, whether your intention is to make your business more profitable, advance in your career or re-organise your life.

The thing that holds them back - this may shock you but it is important for you to know as it will hold YOU back also, is...

Your plan isn't big enough!

Your plan should make your pulse race, make your spine tingle, bring a smile to your face or at least put a bolt-of-lightning enthusiasm into your core. If it doesn't do this then have a rethink.

While your plan doesn't have to be 'big' in the eyes of the world (not everyone wants to run a multinational franchise or be a political leader of their country) it has to be big for you.

So whatever you are planning for your life, your business or your career, ask yourself these questions. Is the dream big? And if it is can you make it bigger?

Top 10 Reasons Why Planning Your Life is Vital

Below is a list of top 10 reasons why planning your life is vital. I have prepared this list to sell you on the fact that you need a plan to get what you want. If you are not yet "sold," read on.

1. **A Planned Life Gives You Direction**. Planning allows you to know where you are going and how you are going to get there. Without a plan, you lack direction and focus and run the risk of spending your time doing things that fail to benefit your future.

2. **A Planned Life Puts Your Dreams Within Reach.** If your dreams have ever felt a little "pie in the sky-ish" it is probably because they were not grounded in a plan. A plan provides action steps necessary to achieve your dreams. Apply the action steps and you are on your way to making your dreams happen.

3. **A Planned Life Puts You In Control.** If you leave your life up to chance or let others control it for you, you are sure to be disappointed. Taking control of your own life is the only way to get what YOU truly want.

4. **A Planned Life Gives You Peace.** Just knowing that you are taking steps to create the life you want gives you a sense of peace. Without a plan, it is easy to get into confusion and despair about which way to go and how to spend your days.

5. **A Planned Life Gives You Purpose.** When you take the time to plan your life you choose to live life "on purpose." You no longer just "exist." You embrace the purpose you were created to fulfil and make it happen through action.

6. **A Planned Life Gives You Passion.** Success is the progressive realization of a worthwhile goal. It is not a destination. It is a journey. When you are headed towards a goal, it makes your "present" more fulfilling, more passionate and exciting.

7. **A Planned Life Empowers You.** Planning puts YOU on YOUR side. When you are single-minded about where you are going, you have power to live your life your way.

8. **A Planned Life Honours God.** You are to be a steward of all God has given you. To manage your life shows that you respect the gift of life that you have been given.

9. **A Planned Life Puts Your Subconscious Mind To Work For You.** When you plan, you plant a vision on your subconscious mind. That vision creates the opportunities for you to succeed at your plan.

10. **A Planned Life Gives You Freedom.** Freedom exists in one place, inside of you. When you claim the freedom you have to shape your destiny, you are truly free.

So How Do You Plan Your Life In The First Place?

There are so many techniques that you can use for planning your ideal life, but the one that works best is when you really and truly know inside and out what you want, how it would look and what it would feel like to be there.

- **Imagine Who You Want To Be**

You can start simply by imagining what you want to be doing on a specific day in the future, for example, 1st January 2020. Flesh out the daily tasks - where are you living, who with and how busy is your day? What do you look like, how do you behave with others and what are your relationships like? All the areas of your life should be included within your plan:

Relationships.

Financial strategies.

Career planning.

 Spiritual planning.

Education.

Entrepreneurship skills.

Friends and Family,

Physical Environment,

Health,

Personal Growth,

Money,

Significant Other,

This is not an exhaustive list - if there is a significant part of your life that is not included above, add another category or rename one.

- **Pay Attention To Detail**

Once you know what you want, it is essential that you break each goal down into smaller ones that you can work towards on a daily basis. For example, if you wish to be healthy enough to run a marathon next year, you could sign up to your local gym today and start going regularly, or find a local running group to join, and then start doing smaller sponsored runs until running is a daily part of your life. Of course, just doing the physical exercise is not the only thing you can do to make this dream come true - for a goal of being healthy, you must also eat healthily, sleep well and enough for you (sleep amounts vary from person to person), be able to manage stress, among many other things.

- **Life Comes Around To Play**

But what happens when you get sucked into the day-to-day drag of life and end up realising that a year has gone by and you haven't done anything towards your goals and you can barely remember what they were in the first place?

What Can You Do With Your Plan When Life Gets In The Way?

- **Be Realistic**

One way that life can get in the way is through sheer overwhelm: you may feel overwhelmed by the sheer size of each category when you do break each big goal from your life plan down into smaller ones. It is really important that you keep motivated and don't ask too much of yourself. If you are asking yourself to do 4 hours worth of work when you only have 30 minutes a day, don't be disheartened, be realistic. You may find that if you set yourself one thing a day to do, and get that done faster than you think then you can get another one done and get ahead of the plan.

- **Be Flexible**

Another way that life can be annoying? is through unexpected twists: this is where keeping your plan flexible comes into play. Depending on what life has thrown at you, there are different ways of doing this. Firstly, you need to keep in control of your plan rather than letting it control you. Monthly, Quarterly and Annual Reviews are very useful ways of making sure your plan fits in with what is really happening in your life and this kind of prevention system can help you anticipate and handle unexpected situations in the best way for you.

- **Be Willing to Reconsider**

What if you change your mind about sections of the plan? No problem - you can redesign your plan as many times as is necessary because it is YOUR plan. Just go back to the drawing board and rethink - you may realise that one change in your plan may impact more areas than the one area you want to alter. It is important to remember here that it is your life and anything is possible, so if the prospect of replanning is daunting, just imagine where you want to be and start taking some action!

- **Be Honest with Yourself**

It is important to know that whatever you plan it must be right for you - if your goal involves actions that you are either not capable of or actions you are not willing to do, you must review what you want and be honest about the likelihood of you actually completing the actions you set yourself.

- **Contemplate a Coach**

What if life keeps getting in the way and you get disheartened about ever having the life you want? Or if you don't have a clue what you want as every situation you try on in your head just doesn't feel right? Here you may have to address your more basic needs and the real situation you're living in. It may be the case that you would benefit from having a coach to help you out in sorting through the top layers of life to the real you underneath - the one which you have hidden away and ignored. A coach can help you realise what your true values are and help you figure out how you can translate this into your current life.

If you do decide to hire a coach, do try a few out to see what different styles are available - most coaches offer a free consultation where you can get to know the personality of the coach and their coaching style before deciding whether it is for you. Prices vary greatly, so this is where trying out many possible coaches can be extremely useful as you can decide whether the service you have just tried is worth the asking price.

- **Proactive & Adaptable**

Life is all about change. How you adapt to that change and how proactive you are in chasing your ideal are what really makes the difference in having a fulfilled life. Having a plan can help you in being prepared for whatever life decides to throw at you while keeping you on track to achieving your dreams.

Develop A Better Future With Eight I Can Do's

1. I Can Move

We live in a global economy. A World where we compete with others across continents and countries- to survive and thrive in this World, we need mobility. Mobility means we can move where the opportunities are, whether they are online or in a place other than we currently call home. This could mean we have to re-focus on the traditional view that a job is where you lay your roots, rather than a successful future is where you are willing to locate.

2. I Can Speak Another Language

Most people from developing Countries learn languages. This is primarily because if you speak more than one language you have more job opportunities. In a global economy, successful people speak and interact in a variety of languages. Mastering a second or third language could enhance your opportunities in the future.

3. I Can Self-Learn

Traditional education is becoming more and more expensive, with Governments cutting back or even increasing the cost of education. Self-learning could bridge this knowledge gap between the ones that can afford an education and those that cannot. On-line education and resources will enhance your knowledge and skills-enabling you to compete globally.

4. I Can Motivate Myself

Motivate yourself to follow and hone in on your interests and skills. Often we can be on our own when we search for new employment or business opportunities, but we do have the resources on hand to nurture these skills. Surf the net for solutions, motivate yourself to focus on the skills you are strong in, see if you can turn an interest into a way to create an income.

5. I Can Have Good Social Networking Skills

Building a social network could enable you to gather new ideas and create new opportunities. It does not mean just selling a product to a friend, but sharing ideas, learning from others in the network and cooperating together to make things better.

6. I Can Save And Invest For My Future

An investment today could be simply building and marketing a website, to buying a set of woodworking tools. The key is to put money aside and see what you can do with these savings. A few hundred dollars could help set you up in a part-time home-based business, whilst a sizeable nest egg in an income-based second home.

7. I Can See What I Really Need

Can you afford to keep up your living standard? If the answer is no, look around at your expenses and what you own, and see if you can make positive cutbacks. A second car could be replaced by a utility vehicle which could help you start a part-time delivery business. If you can't sell it, trade it inside a community trading network- where you get something valuable back, for what was once a financial liability.

8. We Can Give Our Kids A Good Education

Your children need education, but many governments cannot afford to provide a suitable education. The answer could be a homeschooling program, were like-minded neighbours and friends could get together by teaching what you feel is missing in school. This could bridge the growing learning gap in schools, and enhance the quality time you have with your kids.

Understanding The Dreams For A Better Future

In terms of science, dreams are defined as the semi-unconsciousness of mind. It is believed that during sleep, spirits try to give message related to the present & future of an individual. But due to our lack of knowledge, we never understand these signs.

Psychics are the persons who have the exceptional instincts with which they easily understand the messages of the spirits. They use their special powers to understand the paranormal behaviour. With this, they try to bring happiness, wealth, joy & success in the lives of the depressed hearts.

As per psychology, dreams are defined in a different manner. As per famous psychologist Jung, dreams are basically the unfulfilled desires of human beings. He claimed that these represent the mental state of the human beings. With the help of dreams, humans live in the new world where he/she experience various things that are associated with the events that are occurring in life. According to some other psychologists, the dreams have no relevance in the real world. They don't have any significant part to play in the real life of human beings.

But in terms of psychic reading, dreams play a vital role in the life of human beings. These are basically the signs & messages of the spirits that try to say something to an individual about the happening in the future. We all believe that there are certain phenomenon that are beyond the understanding of common man. Some of the activities that take place in our lives are really not controlled by us. So, it is true to say that there are certain forces that are controlling our fate.

Psychics have special vision or instincts. With the help of these instincts, these readers understand & solve the mysteries of life. They provide help to people who seek their help in uncovering the truth about life. They use various methods like candle wax reading, coffee cup reading, etc., to solve the mysteries of life.

Dream interpretation is another method to understand the complexities of life. By using this, method, psychics try to gather information related to the past, present & future of an individual. They believe that in the sleeping state, spirits tries to communicate with an individual.

The spirits give information about the events that will be going to take place in the near future. It is not always necessary that these dreams give information about good fortunes. Many times, some dreams give information about the bad things. These also provide information about the death of a relative or some close person in the near future.

Common persons don't have the ability to interpret the message hidden in dreams. But by telling this, to the psychics an individual can easily get the truth about the hidden meaning. This surely helps in bringing happiness into the lives of millions.

The Power Of Gratitude And Better Future

Can gratitude be a useful way to achieving a better more rewarding life and a positive future? Indeed If you have the power to improve your life based on real thoughts of gratitude, then what things would you want to see in your life?

It has been suggested that the way that you think could have a very important impact on your life. Is it possible that by focusing your thoughts on being grateful for every good thing in your life could have a wonderful powerful life-changing effect on your life. An interesting question is how powerful are your thoughts?

Yes, how really powerful are your thoughts? What if you had the power to transform your life by focusing your attention on gratitude for the good things in your life? Well, that could be quite a powerful gift. Indeed imagine if every time you spent time really thinking about how grateful you are for good things in your life you were able to really bring positive change in your life. That would be a very powerful ability to have, it could mean that as you felt the wonderful feeling of gratitude you would also have positive change.

Should You Focus On The Problems Or On Solutions

It was suggested that anything that you focus on expands, and anything that you do not focus on gets smaller, this is based on a principle called the Law of Attraction. So could this infer that as you think about the problems in your life, they might actually be growing, is there any truth in that. If it is true then it may be a better idea to focus on the good things in your life.

Because if focusing your attention might cause things to grow in your life, then it could perhaps be best to focus your attention on the things that you desire to grow. It may be useful to focus on the life that you are grateful for and the life that you desire to be living. Because perhaps by focusing your attention and time on the positive aspects may allow you to find positive solutions. Indeed, for example, if we were to have the power to influence our environment, then it would be useful to consciously influence it in a positive way. What if your negative thoughts are actually influencing your environment, then that might explain why you get certain results. So if that is true then it might be best to focus on positive results that you desire. What do you think? - Thoughts to make you wonder.

CHAPTER THREE

Planning a perfect lifetime relationship

When your relationship is on the rocks, you will reach a point where you will have to consider whether it is worth saving your relationship. It can be easier to assess the situation if you sit down with a piece of paper and a pencil and really see the strengths and weaknesses in the relationship.

Think About The Following Things:

1. Can you mature with this individual or are you already living separate lives? Roommate situations work for a while but not for a lifelong commitment.

2. Are you both committed to the same goals in life? is it a new house, kids or the beer on Saturday night that is the most important?

3. Do each of you actually know what happiness means to the other person? Is it no bills or a long-awaited trip? Could it be the ball game on Saturday night?

There are two times that people put the most effort into a relationship--at the beginning, and at the end. At the beginning, we want so much to spend time together that we will make time to do whatever it takes. At the end of a relationship, we spend a lot of effort just to keep ourselves together while our relationship is falling apart. Many people learn too late that the most important time to work on a relationship is . . . every day. Because, while choosing a good partner is essential, just committing to someone does not ensure years of happiness.

To continue to reap the rewards of a great relationship, there is a continual amount of work that must be done. Just as a farmer cannot sow his seeds and sit back until they mature, so it is that we cannot expect an initial commitment to carry us to a great relationship.

The Importance Of Developing Good Relationships

Research has shown that good relationships make life worth living. This is because you tend to enjoy life. This is as a result of having people to share your problems with.

For example, if you are facing financial, family, and social problems, you have people to talk to about the problems that you are going through. This aids in lightening the burden.

Sharing also aids in taking away the sense that you are the only one who is suffering. This acts as a stress buster which ensures that you are happy and you enjoy your life.

Healthy relationships also play a huge role in increasing one's productivity. This is linked to the fact that if you are in a healthy relationship, you tend to be less stressed; therefore, you are able to concentrate in your career or business.

Due to this, you are able to focus and put in long hours in your work which greatly increases your productivity.

If it's in the workplace, you tend to focus on your work and as a result, you are easily promoted to higher positions.

Good relationships tend to give you a lot of freedom and positive energy. This is because instead of spending time and energy on overcoming problems that are associated with negative emotions brought about by negative relationships, you focus on opportunities that are available for you.

For example, if you are a business owner, having negative emotions can deter you from seeing viable business opportunities.

When you are in a good relationship you tend to have a clear mind; therefore, you are able to see any opportunities that might be available for you and as a result, you take advantage of them at the right time. This plays a huge role in bringing about expansion and growth of your business.

Important Factors Of Good Relationships

Relationships are the most important aspect of life, much more important than money and financial security. A rich man that does not enjoy good relationship would live an empty life, even with his abundant finances. A good relationship brightens up life, and a poor one makes life feel very sad and meaningless. There are a few factors that will push relationship up the right track.

The First Would Be Trust. If trust does not exist between 2 persons, then the relationship cannot be a fulfilling one. Maybe it wouldn't go down, bit it certainly would not go up. There is no trust without honesty and transparency. When both parties are comfortable of being open with each other, and always say the truth, regardless of situations, then a culture of trust is solid between the two. That means saying what you mean, whether you are happy or upset. There is no relationship worse than one where trust is non-existent.

Secondly, know to play the game of the balance of power. Power exists in all relationships: parents and children, superior and subordinate, teacher and student, friends and couples. Power exists anywhere, between any. Power could be defined as how one behaves when faced with another person. For example, a military officer would have more power than a subordinate, when it comes to speech and everything. Likewise, in the case of couples, the balance of power can be shifted according to situation. Giving power requires respect and self-control. A great play of power balance will make a good relationship.

Last But Equally As Important, a good relationship requires both parties to compromise for each others' sake. Because every one of us views the world in their own lenses, it's not too uncommon to find a point where you would disagree with each other. Then, you would need to solve the problem in one out of 2 ways. The first is to quarrel. This is very immature and hurts that love that exists. The second is to take a step back and compromise. This should be the ideal way disagreements should ever be solved. A quarrel is an example of a lose-lose situation, so it's not wise to blow up.

Reasons Relationships Fail And How To Succeed

The most common reasons given for the failure of relationships are sex, money and time issues. It usually a combination of these and other factors that result in divorce or calling it quits. Although the divorce rate has decreased slightly over the last few years, this can largely be attributed to more people choosing to live together rather than getting married. And of those who live together, there is a higher "turnover rate" than that of married couples. So if you are looking for a lasting relationship, marriage is still the gold standard. Listed below are the top ten reasons why relationships fail. By becoming aware of the warning signs and making the necessary changes you will have a better chance of making it to "happily ever after."

1. **Lost That Loving Feeling** –

When we first meet someone that we are attracted to we are under the influence of a powerful cocktail of sex hormones. First, you are hit with blast of testosterone and estrogens which create that initial "he/shes hot". Next, we are slammed with increased levels of the neurotransmitters adrenaline, dopamine and serotonin. And if that is not enough preparation for surges of the attachment hormones oxytocin and vasopressin. So what does all of this have to do with why relationships fail? Well, basically for anywhere from 12 to 24 months you are hijacked by your hormones and lost in that "loving feeling." Once the hormone levels return to normal, (which unfortunately they always do) couples start to see all of the little imperfections in their partner.

Partners can begin to feel more like roommates or even adversaries than lovers. That special someone that made us "so happy" now seems to be the target of our indifference or frustrations. We start holding each other responsible for our needs, wants and desires. We tend to stop putting in the energy and effort to please each other and become more and more aware of our unmet needs from childhood which usually leads to blaming, nagging, distancing and seeking other sources of gratification. This is where awareness, insight, communication and dedication to your relationship come into play. There are ways to increase your "love hormones" and get that "Loving Feeling" back.

2. Poor Communication –

55% of all communication is through body language. So those crossed arms, turned away body, avoiding eye contact, tense muscles, pursed lips, raised eyebrows, etc speak volumes. Learn to be aware of the messages you are sending and receiving from your partner. The tone, speed and volume of your voice account for 35% of communication. That extra pause you take before answering or the slightly raised or lowered voice, as well as "that tone" all speak volumes to your partner. Only 10% of communication is based on the words you are actually speaking to your partner.

The first step is to become aware of how you are communicating on all three levels and learn some simple techniques to mirror, validate, and empathize with your partner. When couples stop talking and become distant or start attacking and blaming without ever resolving issues the relationship begins to break down. We all want to feel heard, know that we make sense and that we are understood.

3. Financial Problems –

Money matters, but often not in the ways couples think it may. There is a bit of truth in the old saying "He with the Gold Rules", so rule gently. Money can create control, power struggles, and resentment in relationships. Often, however, it is not so much about the dollars spent as it is about understanding each other's attachment and feelings around money. And yes, we all have strong, even primal feelings about money. So, if you are a Saver and your partner is a Spender it may feel like your partner's spending is an assault on you. Instead of realizing that you and your partner may have a very different relationship with money, individuals often feel like their partner does not care about their feelings - their need for security, or their need to enjoy life via that new car, dress, or sumptuous fine dining experience. Couples are in trouble when they start omitting purchases, hiding them from one another or squirrelling away money behind their partners back.

Over time it gets easier and easier to justify these little deeds/deceptions which will ultimately break the trust in your relationship. It is important that couples discuss and learn about each others spending style and then create a budget that embraces the styles of both partners.

4. Lack of Time –

Quality Time that is. In this day and age of high tech communication more and more couples find themselves working longer hours, working from or while at home, and during the evening and on weekends. Couples often complain about their partner spending too much time answering emails, texting and chatting with others while supposedly spending 'quality time' together. Whether it is being addicted to work, technology or the introduction of children to the marriage, the time that was once spent with our partner now takes a back seat. Initially, our partner was our number one priority and we spent a great deal of time with them and thinking about them. As the saying goes "Show me where you spend your time and money and I will tell you what is important to you." Without quality time together couples grow further and further apart. Make time for your relationship. Plan mutually enjoyable activities at the top of your "to do list" and do them regularly.

5. Sexual Issues –

Sex. Not having it, not having enough of it, having it with someone else or even something else, i.e. the internet, causes major problems in relationships. The bottom line is that a marriage without sex represents deeper unresolved issues in the relationship. If you are having sexual issues in your relationship you are not alone: over 50% of couples report having sexual problems and approximately 15% of couples report having sexless relationships. Most relationships with sexual issues eventually end in divorce. Therefore, unless you want to be fighting over who gets the fine china, it is important to stop avoiding this elephant in the room and discuss it with your partner or seek help if this feels too uncomfortable.

6. Marrying too Young –

Women that marry before the age of 25 are twice as likely to get divorced than women who marry after the age of 25. In general, couples that are older have a better idea of who they are and what they want in life. They also have better communication skills and tend to be more established in their careers. If you are under 25 and you have met that special someone, not all is doomed. It is important that as you mature as a couple you address life issues and goals as they come up and make adjustments to your relationship as a couple.

7. Loss of Respect and Admiration –

When couples stop admiring each other and begin treating each other with disrespect the relationship slowly erodes. Spiteful words, name-calling and attacking one's character have long-lasting if not irreversible consequences on the relationship. Like a wall that is built one brick at a time each unfair argument and cutting word builds a barrier of distrust, resentment and anger in the relationship. If couples stop showing respect and admiration for each other what do they have left? We all want to be respected and admired and when we are not, we shut down and pull away.

After years of verbal abuse, most couples call it quits. It is important that couples learn how to fight fair expressing their feelings without attacking and blaming their partner. It is important that you ask for what you need in the relationship and listens to what your partner needs as well. We often take our partners' admirable traits for granted. Couples need to continue to admire each other and voice their admiration every day.

8. Opposites Attract and Butt-Heads –

Yes, many of us are initially attracted to people that are different from ourselves. If we are a bit shy, we love their exuberant outgoing personality, however, this love and admiration for the differences can turn into an annoying misunderstanding of their personality. We may find ourselves saying things like, "Why can't they calm down and quit talking to anyone who will listen." If we are outgoing and free-spirited, we may initially love their responsible and stable attitude, but later feel controlled and defensive. Unfortunately, this initial attraction later sets the stage for many of our issues with our partner.

Different values, different ideas of how to live our lives quickly leads to anger, defensiveness and a slow fracturing of the love affair. When you find yourself attracted to and ultimately falling in love with an opposite, realize that this is what has drawn you to this person. It is important to look a little deeper. Why are you shy and what does it mean if you are the life of the party? Or if you are footloose and fancy-free, what does it mean to have boundaries and structure? It is also important to look at these differences and realize they add spice and or balance to your life and appreciate them.

9. Poor Boundaries with Extended Family –

Be it in-laws, siblings, step-children, ex-husbands or your own children, they all come into play when it comes to creating stress on your relationship. Being able to take time for yourselves as a couple, minus the other members of your family is crucial to sustaining a loving relationship. Supporting each other as a couple and as a united front, rather than letting the in-laws or the children overrun your partner is an important part in keeping the respect alive. As much as children are "bundles of joy" many studies show that couples without children are happier. Now that is not to say children are not a "blessed gift." It is to say that they add stress to the relationship. Setting boundaries for your relationship, such as standing up for your partner and agreeing on the modes of discipline used for your children or step-children will keep your relationship strong and resilient. The best relationships resemble a pyramid with the "happy bride and groom" at the top.

10. Substance and Alcohol Abuse-

These can destroy relationships one drink, one pill or one puff at a time. A dependence on any substance will be a distraction from true intimacy and romance. Unfortunately, the abuser is more in love with the substance than their partner. If the abuse continues, and the sober partner stays, feelings of resentment and anger become toxic and possibly irreversible to the relationship. Standing by your partner while they are engaging in substance abuse, is setting the precedence for how other dynamics will be played out in the partnership.

When one person is high you are living in two different realities never truly connecting. Asking your partner to seek help for their dependence, setting limits and establishing time frames for recovery will create the respect for yourself and your relationship.

Steps in Building Great Soulmate Relationships

Building great soulmate relationships in life takes time and commitment. If you choose to spend time and you choose to commit you will most certainly build a relationship that will bring you joy and contentment. Some keys to building great relationships include:

- **Connect With The One That You Love**

Make time to remind your soulmate that they are special. Write them a note, send an email, SMS or phone them during the day at work. Do something that you know will be meaningful to your partner. Make sure your efforts don't go to waste; connect with them keeping their love language in mind. Be intentional about making a daily connection in the middle of your busy life.

- **Plan Your Time**

The old saying 'fail to plan and you will plan to fail' is so true when it comes to soulmate relationships. Planning your time is of utmost importance in building great soulmate relationships. The average couple is so busy with work, catching up with friends and other responsibilities that sometimes in an established relationship you can fail to plan to spend time together. Check your calendars each week and make note of time when you will be together. Be intentional about spending casual social time together and also about spending quality time building into your soulmate relationship. A regular 'date night' is a great idea.

- **Be Protective Of Your Soulmate Relationship**

At times healthy jealousy is a must in relationships. If you are not going to protect your soulmate relationship, who will? Don't allow yourself to be in situations that compromise the integrity of your relationship with your partner. Always remember that soulmate relationship can last forever- make sure that the emotional needs of your partner are being met. Don't take each other for granted. Your relationship is important.

- **Don't Forget The Special Occasions!**

Use your diary or the reminder function in your mobile phone; make a note of birthdays, anniversaries and special events. Talk about important events and make sure that both partners' expectations are equal. Unnecessary tension can result in a relationship due to unmet expectations. If you would like to go away for your anniversary make sure that your partner knows! They are not minding readers. It may seem to take the spontaneity and romance out of it all but in the long run, your soulmate relationship will be stronger as a result of discussing such issues.

- **Introduce Surprise To Your Relationship**

Assuming your partner likes surprises, and you have time, there are many ways you can surprise them. Organise with their boss that they will take an extended lunch break and take them out to lunch, send flowers, a card, chocolates- the options are endless and can really add spice to your life together. Interrupt the mundane with a surprise and you'll be amazed at what it does for your soulmate relationship.

- **Get Away With Your Friends**

If you are in a steady relationship make sure that you haven't become exclusive with your partner and in the process lost all of your friends! This is a common mistake that couples make when entering into a relationship. At the start, everything is new and very exciting and before you know it you have neglected the old friend that you have had since high school. Friendships are important and it is healthy to have mutual friends and for each person to have their own friends in a relationship. It brings diversity and spending time apart only makes the heart grow fonder!

- **Become A Student Of Your Partner**

If you are in a relationship you need to become a full-time student of your partner. Make it your mission to learn everything there is to know about them. Their likes, dislikes, strengths, weaknesses, how they relate to others, how they feel most loved.

When you take the focus off yourself and your needs and focus on your partner you will discover that you are in the process of building a great relationship. As you focus on your partner they will become more focused on you- it is always better to give than to receive!

9 Restorative Good Relationship Moments

I want to share with you what I think are nine restorative relationship moments.

1. **Intimacy** - good relationships feature intimacy, which I define as vulnerability shared courageously in the closeness of trust. Our trust empowers another to trust, and that mutual permission grants access to freedom for both we call respect.

2. **Meeting** - all good relationships require a meeting. But just the same there are times when we should continue to meet when the relationship faces trials, We all want to back out of moments when meeting takes courage - where meeting will involve confrontation.

3. **Confrontation** - none of us enjoys being confronted, and not many of us enjoy confronting, but good confrontations - where both parties feel empowered because they're safe - is so important for relationship happiness. Confrontations implicit of love show that caring is an extension of the truth because love ensures that the confrontation is productive. Love neither does not give up nor give in.

4. **Listening** - no list on good relationship moments would be complete without the word listening. We see it practised so rarely, and we may hardly experience it. But, if we can be the ones who can start by listening well enough to understand, our relationships will be all better for it. Listening properly requires great faith to leave aside our needs to serve another person's first.

5. **Apology** - I'm a big fan of Dr Gary Chapman's five Languages of Apology, for we all speak 'sorry' differently. Every great relationship requires every person to apologise. Apology precipitates forgiveness.

6. **Forgiveness** - such a complex subject comprising a plethora of relationship moments. Forgiveness is God's grace, redoubled in human form.

7. **Restoration** - transactions of forgiveness are fundamental to restoration.

8. **Triumph** - such a moment is only known beyond the pain of a difficulty reconciled, where both parties add the significant effort of humility to

overcome their differences. There can be no triumph moment where one person exudes all the humility, and the other encamps in pride.

9. **Exemplification** - as two are exemplars of these great relationship moments, a moment is created where others learn.

CHAPTER FOUR

Financial planning for a better tomorrow

People who strive hard will certainly receive rewards. Without a doubt, everyone can reach their goals if they are determined, responsible, and intelligent. If you really want to reach your goal to achieve success, then you should know how to deal with the challenges in life. In business, you need to understand the purpose of what you are managing. You need to be familiar with the possible pros and cons of a certain undertaking that you intend to engage in. Dealing with monetary issues is a crucial task. In order to succeed, you need to have an effective financial planning. It is necessary to take the right steps so that you will not slip into the financial hellhole.

If you think that you are not expert enough when it comes to budgeting, securing your earnings, and to increase your profits then the best thing that you should do is to hire a professional and trustworthy fiscal advisor. Certainly, no one wants to lose their valuable assets. It is important for you to know how to properly manage your wealth so that you and your family will have a brighter tomorrow. We all want to have a prosperous life; hence, we need to seek a solution that could deliver beneficial outcomes concerning financial matters.

Indeed, we are the ones who decide for our future. Although we cannot predict what will happen in the following years, we still have ways on how to be prepared for it. In terms of economic issues, you must look for ways on how to avoid the possible dilemmas that we might encounter. In case of emergencies, you will easily have something to use if you have a contingency plan. Nothing can stop you from achieving your business goals as long as you know how to manage financial issues.

It will be easy for you to increase your business' sales and profits if you have done the right monetary planning. You should practice doing a systematic approach to any tasks that you are going to do so that you will obtain a surefire and successful outcome.

Common Mistakes People Make Affecting Financial Plan

The most 10 common mistakes people make which will affect financial freedom:-

1. **Under Save:** Without a financial plan, how do you estimate how much you need to support your financial goals and commitments? You might erroneously think that you can afford to spend most, if not all, of your current income.

2. **Over Save:** Some people tend to underspend and save a lot of their income. Believing that saving more will have better financial position during retirement. However, this is might be half true. We need to save just sufficient money to meet our financial goals and not just for the sake of saving. You need to have financial plan to determine your optimal saving amount.

3. **Under Insure, Or Over Insure:** Every one of you might have different protection needs, it is hard to determine how much you should insure

yourself if you don't have a clear financial situation. You might over insure if you are risk averse or under insure if you are a risk taker.

4. **Buy Big Property Such House And Car:** Most people will determine whether they can afford their home by looking at their ability to pay the down payment and service the monthly mortgage instalments. However, do you think about how the purchase will affect your ability to achieve future financial goals? With a proper financial plan, you will be able to identify the real price you affordable for that home or car purchase. You will be able to adjust your expenses such as children's tertiary education, your retirement age, your retirement income and other financial goals to accommodate your purchase.

5. **Overspend Or Under Spend:** Without proper financial plan, you can't see the impact of your children's tertiary education funding on your other financial goals. The idea is not to overspend on one child and affect the funding of other financial goals or worse, the funding of others children's tertiary education. On the other hand, you don't want to underspend on your children's tertiary education and regret it later.

6. **Invest In Unsuitable Investment Products:** Without a proper financial plan, you won't be able to identify the investment on return (ROI) that suit your financial freedom. You may end up investing in wrong investment products which might affect your financial plan.

7. **Over-Invest In Properties:** With a financial plan, you will have to think about diversifying your asset allocation; without a plan, you may end up investing only in properties. Property investment is not bad but overinvesting will expose you to too much risk in one asset class and badly affect your portfolio if the property sector takes a dip. it may also affect your cash flow if you take out too many mortgages.

8. **Undersell Your Business:** Selling your business at a good price can give you financial freedom and a worry-free retirement. Without a financial plan, you might risk underselling your business.

9. **Retire Too Early Or Too Late:** In retirement planning, you don't want to retire too early and end up not having enough financial resources to support your retirement lifestyle. You also don't want to retire too late that you might don't have enough time to enjoy life.

10. **Planning And Slow Acting:** Without a financial plan, you don't know the exact price you will be paying for procrastination --- either in saving, investing or insuring. You might take it easy until it is too late.

What Should Be In Your Plan?

Here are the main areas which need to be covered. There may be other areas, depending on your own circumstances.

- **Gathering Data**

You need to think of your plan as a whole because your financial decisions are inter-linked. For example, if you have an expensive mortgage this may impact on your ability to save for the future. You will need to get together data on every aspect of your financial situation.

- **Setting Goals**

Without an end in mind, it will be difficult to evaluate your progress. Therefore you should think carefully about what you want your future to look like. These goals should be measurable.

- Income And Outgoings

This is fundamental to building your plan. If you spend less than you earn, you have a chance to affect your financial future. If you spend more than you earn you will have limited options and could spiral into debt. Understanding tax is a big part of this.

- Assets And Liabilities

You need to build up assets to underpin your financial future. And more importantly, you need to build up the right kinds of assets. The sooner you can be debt free (unless it is the 'right debt'), the sooner you can be in control. For planning purposes, we ignore certain types of assets.

Emergency Funding

Making sure you can cope with short-term crises is vital. We recommend that you set aside 3-6 months worth of outgoings.

- Protecting What You Have Got

You should think about what happens if things go wrong. This includes all types of insurance to ensure your lifestyle is defended by catastrophes. You should also consider making wills and powers of attorney etc.

- Paying Off Debt

Generally, any debt is a barrier to your future prosperity. The sooner you become debt free, the sooner you have control over your future. Remember that your bank manager includes your mortgage as one of his assets!

- **Saving For The Future And Investing Wisely**

You need to work out how much will be needed to fund your future goals, how much risk this requires, and the effect of external forces such as inflation, charges and future legislation.

- **Tax**

While this should not drive your plan, it is certainly an important part of the equation. Understanding how tax affects your life should run throughout your plan.

- **Monitoring Your Progress**

Financial planning should be much like servicing your car. You would not spend £20,000 on a new car and then never take it to the garage for a service. Likewise, you should regularly review your plan to ensure you remain on target to meet your goals.

Of course, your circumstances will also change over time, so your ultimate goals may also need a tweak from time to time.

Important Steps in Financial Planning

There are three main aspects to financial planning: Budgeting and saving; investing; and retirement and estate planning. You must work on all three in order to have a balanced financial picture.

There is no way around it. No matter how much you dislike the idea, budgeting is one of the main requirements of successfully managing your finances. It isn't the negative task that many people assume it to be. It isn't a financial diet and it isn't something that deprives you of the things you want.

Today, when most people hear the word "budget", it readily implies a negative connotation. They think that budgeting is only for those experiencing financial shortage or crisis. However, even with enough financial resources as of the moment, an effective financial planning program will ensure that you will be able to maintain your financial status.

Therefore, financial budgeting involves the following:

i.   Financial budget for your day-to-day finances while not depriving yourself of what provides you enjoyment and satisfaction.

ii. Setting up larger financial goals to which your daily budget and planning is aim towards.

iii. Making sure that you have enough savings in case of emergencies or unexpected financial struggles.

The Importance of Budget

Others think that by creating a budget for your finances, it is similar to lack of financial freedom. However, it is of the exact opposite. By creating a budget, you are able to create a financial safety net so you have enough money to spend on things that you want without hurting your financial condition.

Regardless of how little or large you earn on a monthly or yearly basis, budget enables you to take an effective step towards a healthier financial foundation. Hence, you can easily realize whatever financial goals you have.

When making a budget, it is important to keep track of every detail in your expenses - even up to the last cent. Hence, you can also evaluate your spending habits. It allows you to determine whether you are placing your money on important things or whether you can do without it.

Too many people assume that investing is something that is out of their reach. However, investing is vital in preparing for your future. All you have to do is educate yourself and get started. You don't have to have a lot of money to invest. The key is to start investing and let your money grow over time.

Investing is one of the best ways to prepare for your retirement. If you want to retire comfortably, it is never too early to begin planning. You probably want to enjoy your life during retirement. Without wise planning, you could spend most of your golden years working. Social Security may not be there when you reach retirement age. If it is, it probably won't be enough to maintain your current lifestyle.

With proper planning, retirement can be something to look forward to. Along with planning for retirement and getting your estate in order, you need to have proper insurance to cover any emergencies that could pop up. Good health insurance and generous life insurance should be top priorities. You should also have property insurance that covers all hazards in your area. If you can afford it, disability insurance is always a good idea.

You can change the way you are living. You can create a financial peace for your family. All it takes is the proper financial planning. Just start with one step today. You will find that it won't be long until you have everything together.

Stabilize Your Current Situation Before You Invest

Before you consider investing in any type of market, you should really take a long hard look at your current situation. Investing in the future is a good thing, but clearing up bad - or potentially bad - situations in the present is more important.

Pull your credit report. You should do this once each year. It is important to know what is on your report and to clear up any negative items on your credit report as soon as possible. If you've set aside $25,000 to invest, but you have $25,000 worth of bad credit, you are better off cleaning up the credit first!

Next, look at what you are paying out each month, and get rid of expenses that are not necessary. For instance, high-interest credit cards are not necessary. Pay them off and get rid of them. If you have high-interest outstanding loans, pay them off as well.

If nothing else, exchange the high-interest credit card for one with lower interest and refinance high-interest loans with loans that are lower interest. You may have to use some of your investment funds to take care of these matters, but in the long run, you will see that this is the wisest course of action. Get yourself into good financial shape - and then enhance your financial situation with sound investments.

It doesn't make sense to start investing funds if your bank balance is always running low or if you are struggling to pay your monthly bills. Your investment dollars will be better spent to rectify adverse financial issues that affect you each day.

While you are in the process of clearing up your present financial situation, make it a point to educate yourself about the various types of investments. This way, when you are in a financially sound situation, you will be armed with the knowledge that you need to make equally sound investments in your future.

The Best Mortgage Deal For You And Your Current Situation And How To Get It!

There are many different types of mortgage and the trick when it comes to refinancing, purchasing a home, or getting any type of mortgage is finding the best mortgage deal for you and your situation. There is a lender out there that has the solution to your issue, and you just have to know how to find this lender so that you can use them to accomplish your current goals.

The first place you can start is with your current mortgage company and get a quote from them in writing. Sure this will not be true if you are trying to purchase a home unless you currently own one, but if you are looking to refinance, take out a second mortgage, or get a home equity loan, then starting with your current company is a great way to go.

The second place you should look for the best mortgage deal for you is right online. This is a great way to do some very quick and easy comparison shopping. You will want to know how much your home will appraise for and how much you currently owe on it. This is important because if you have these numbers wrong then any online quotes you get will also be wrong.

The last place to look is with a mortgage broker. This is not a bad option, but you usually pay a little more in fees because this is a service they are going to provide you. They will search through numerous companies for you and help find the right deal that fits you perfectly. They will help you get exactly what you are after and will do most of the legwork for you.

How To Use Your Current Situation To Make Money Online

One thing that does catch people off-guard is how they can make money on the Internet starting with none. On the opposite end of the spectrum. it is surprising how many people already have enough money, but really lack time.

Initially, you have to answer the question do you have more time or money to build an Internet business. The one thing that is beautiful about the Internet is how you can benefit regardless of your current situation.

How else can you explain a 13-year-old living in Thailand who is earning a six-figure income online. Or an 80-year-old grandma who supplements her retirement income with an additional $300 a month on the Internet.

The key is to not let your current situation determine what you need to make money online. Rather what you have to do is understand how to utilize the hand that you've been dealt to get where you want to be.

Let me give you a couple of specific examples.

There are people building Internet businesses online today who do virtually none of the work themselves. What they do is outsourcing almost everything. The beauty of the Internet is that you can find someone who is willing to do almost anything if you'll pay them.

You can find these people in discussion forums, on websites like eLance.com, and various other ways. The key is that if you have money, you can still build a fantastic Internet business and pay to have it done.

Now looks look at the flipside of this. There are people who come online every day wanting to make money, and yet have nothing to get started with. That is okay, but these people have to understand the amount of work that is going to take to overcome this obstacle.

Getting traffic to a moneymaking website is the key and yet how are you going to do that if you have nothing to invest in advertising. You must learn how to promote online for free or nearly free.

This is more of a get rich slow approach, but in the long run can be very effective if you do it properly. There are many examples of people who now earn full-time incomes and even excellent part-time incomes online doing things that they started part-time.

Examples of what you may have to do initially yourself would include article writing, submitting articles, submitting your website by hand to directories, posting in blogs, participating in discussion forums, placing classified ads in directories, and so on.

If you're willing to buckle down and go to work, regardless of whether you have money now or not, you can make money online. And of course, as we stated, if you have more money than you have time, you can build a fantastic business as well.

CHAPTER FIVE

Career planning - your guide to a successful future!

Having a career plan is a useful tool to monitor your career progress. It cannot be overemphasized the importance of having a realistic workable career plan. The operative words here are that you work the plan. You monitor your career progress and over time you make adjustments to your career plan as circumstances change.

Why then do so many neglects something that is an indispensable component to success? Here may be a few reasons why many neglect this key element to finding and growing their careers.

Many are afraid of failing. They may consider and start career planning, but they fail to implement their plan, and at the first sign of a lack of success they stop the process. They also may set their sights way out of reach. When their goals are not met they blame the plan and all activity stops.

Others with an abundance of experience conclude they have no need to create a career plan. This approach may work around the edges but to achieves something more meaningful experience will not replace a well thought out career plan.

On the other side of experience those with little practical experience and who, "don't know what they don't know," and are moved by events outside their control. They never take the time to learn what is involved in career planning.

Finally, the major reason is laziness. Effective career planning is work. It takes thinking, research and continued effort. It can't be an infre⬛uent activity.

Successfully managing your own career is critical for your financial and personal well being. Yet it is rarely pursued on a strategic or informed basis. Career planning, particularly in the technology field, is more and more the responsibility of the individual. Particularly, since most people, today end up working for many employers.

The overall basis for more successful career management includes developing plans that are applicable at different stages in your working life. And even more important if you plan on a career change after 50.

Although living in the information age, there are few comprehensive job information and planning resources available online. Exploring a career versus job information is more readily available once you have focused on a career path, such as technology or even further, within a specific industry.

When employed the employer generally provides training, successive jobs, and a defined career ladder to the degree that it unites with the organization's needs and objectives. Outplacement counsellors generally help people focus on job searches rather than career plans. Recruiters are looking to fill job positions with top candidates for employers who are their clients and normally do not provide career planning services for individuals.

We can generally fit career planning as having three major phases: early stage from ages 16 to 33; middle, from 34 to 52; and later, beyond 53. Many times, early career choices are highly influenced by parents, relatives, and teacher's or close friends. The choices of technical schools, colleges or graduate schools, as well as majors, begin to focus interests for career paths.

It is important, in the early stages of a career planning, to carefully make choices, as initial decisions can have a major impact on long-term career success and ultimately, happiness.

Mid-stage career planning and effort usually reflect the initial experiences and jobs one has had with his or her early career. It generally is an extension of that experience. At this stage, there may be a thread of a career track, but job moves and knowledge growth during this phase that are not well planned or executed can result in important limits to career-growth.

Late-stage career planning frequently results from the need to find the right position in one's career after an early retirement or a reduction in force. After 50 career planning at this stage generally reflects more entrepreneurial, part-time, or flexible working arrangements. This is when traditional employment limitations, as well as long developed interests, come more into focus.

Critical Mistakes To Avoid In Career Planning

You may have read what Brian Tracy said about developing career goals, "An average person with average talent, ambition and education, can outstrip the most brilliant genius in our society if that person has clearly focused goals."

Why then do more people make mistakes at career planning? What do they not do to manage working out a career plan?

First, they have unrealistic goals. They do not break the individual career goal down to manageable bites. If they plan on reading 100 books in two years, it does them little good trying to read all the books in the last weekend before the end of the two years. A manageable goal, for example, would be to read two books a month. You can measure it at the end of the month and adjust it as you go along. More likely with this approach you'll reach and exceed the overall goal of 200 books read in two years.

Also, unrealistic aspirations become more realistic if you check the goals out with your mentors and friends. Moreover, unrealistic career goals are rarely met so the individual gets discouraged and the overall plan becomes ignored and useless.

Second, many work out career plans that have a limited range and scope. They view themselves as only working in one job or type of job. This restricts career options dramatically and can have an effect on reducing overall job satisfaction. Expand your horizons, and work hard to cross-train in other related careers. Learn other skills and you'll find other opportunities opening for you.

Third, a career plan that is over detailed and leaves no room or time to respond to changes in external or internal circumstances could become a problem. Further, having a laundry list of detailed action items usually means a lack of priorities. This leads to little or no effective action on the career plan.

Fourth, a career plan that depends on others to recognize your skills and potential is doomed to failure. Developing a plan that re□uires your organization to plan the development and advancement of your career is going in the wrong direction.

Career planning and development is your responsibility and your responsibility alone. Your organization may provide resources but it is your responsibility to take the required actions to plan and develop your career.

Fifth, many take unnecessary risks in their lack of career planning. They do not develop proper options nor develop the basic skills and understandings re□uired to move to the next level or to properly prepare themselves to change careers.

You should be making informed choices, with proper preparation to assure your career plan develops the planned results.

So we have five main areas that many do not do in planning and managing their careers:

(1) They set unrealistic goals;

(2) Their career plans have limited range and scope;

(3) They have an overly detailed career plan;

(4) Their career plan depends on others; and

(5) Their lack of a career plan mean they take unnecessary risks with their career and their future.

Factors Involved in Career Planning and Development

There are several reasons that constitute career planning and development.

1. **You Will Be Able To Set Yourself Goals.** Setting goals and aims is an imperative part of career planning. The improvement in your career will gradually start to become visible once you start setting yourself goals, which can either be short term or long term. You will be more focused on your effort to taste success in your career by setting yourself goals. As a result, it is more likely that you will be getting into a good position in your profession by setting yourself goals.

2. **A Plan Will Help You A Great Deal For Your Career.** You will be able to control the development in your career by crafting a deft career plan. An

overall progress in your career can be observed when you start to lay emphasis towards your career goals and objectives.

3. **You Will Also Be Able To Maintain A Competitive Edge Above Your Competitors In Your Field By Designing A Good Career Development Plan.** Your new skills and additional certifications will assist you in staying a cut above the rest and at the top along with your abilities and educational qualifications. It is well-known fact that individuals with additional skills are bound to contribute more to the development of the company and in turn also end up earning more than his/her professional peers.

4. **It Will Become Imminent That You Are Keen On Improving Your Capabilities And Knowledge By Having A Career Development Plan.** As a result, your future employers will become more interested in you because of your aspiration for higher education and self-improvement. It is common knowledge that employers opt for individuals who are constantly looking to develop themselves as assets.

Is It Time To Quit Your Current Job?
Signs That Mean It's Time To Leave Your Current Job

You are thinking of quitting your job. But resigning from your current job should not be a decision make haphazardly though, because it may have big impact on your life. You should think carefully and take various factors into consideration before you finalize your decision and submit your resignation letter to your superior. Here are some situations that may trigger the right time for you to go for a new job:

1. Your Job Makes You Sick

You feel overwhelming stresses on your current job and it makes feel headaches and backaches. You are trying very hard to work out the problem but unfortunately, you failed. You are losing your sleep and impacting your health and living norm. Under this situation, you probably want to prioritize your health first by finding a new job and change to new working environment.

2. You Have Been Marginalized

You have been taken away many of your responsibilities without any reason. Your boss does not trust you like before anymore. You are excluded from important meetings and just being assigned with unimportant works that will only contribute very little scores on your year-end job evaluation for promotion or salary increment. You should talk to your boss to find out the reasons before you do anything, but be aware that your boss may be urging you to leave. If the situation seems like won't improve, then it may be the right time to take the hint and find a new job.

3. You Receive A Better Offer Elsewhere

If you are given opportunities, you definitely want to move to as higher level as possible in your career which enables you to enjoy better income and lifestyle. Along with our career path, there will be many opportunities opened to you and if you get an offer that attracts you very much and the prospective position seems to be a good fit for you, then you should give it a serious consideration.

4. You Have Outgrown Your Job Requirement

You have gained a lot of experience in your current job and you find that your experience is beyond your job requirement but there is no opportunity for you to move up and no room for you to utilize your experience. Then, you probably need to find the opportunity elsewhere.

5. Your Job Is Interfering With Your Family Obligations

Sometimes it's hard to balance between job and family, but with some scarification and tolerance, many parents still able to achieve some degree of balancing between their job and their family obligations. But, if your job requires you to spend too much of your time and cause you losing focus on your family obligations, then you might want to find other job that has fixed working schedule or consider an alternative work option like working from home.

In summary, quitting job or change job is a norm for one's career life, but if you are thinking of quitting your current job due to any reason, don't make haphazardly decision until you have considered all potential impacts on your life.

How To Create Your Unique Career Plan

A career plan can be whatever you want it to be. It can be a short-term or a long-term plan, or both. That is the beauty of it; you get to decide. It is your plan.

There is no handy GPS to direct you back to the right road. You have to solve your confusion by developing a strong career plan with a career map leading you out of the wilderness. To get back on course it's critical to find the road to wanting to travel along with your destination.

You don't immediately have to have a final career destination, right down to the street address. But getting into the right zip code will allow you the flexibility to fine-tune your career plan as you get closer to your final career objectives.

Here are the four fundamental factors you should review as you design a map to get your career plan back on track.

1. **Where Are You Now?** Just like zeroing in on a computer-based satellite map there will be a proper distance where everything becomes clearer. Being able to see your entire career path up to this point is important to keep things in perspective.

What factors in a career are most important to you? Where do you want to work? What type and size of an organization best fit your interests? Is self-employment a possibility? Future aspects of the career: salary, promotion how important are they?

How far down the road will you be looking? One year maybe up to three to five years or longer depending on the destination should be how detailed you build your career plan.

2. **Self-Assessment Leads To Self-Improvement.** One critical element in the development of a career plan is a self-assessment. A self-evaluation is extremely important because it leads to a self-understanding. Socrates was right when he pleaded, "know yourself." Self-understanding is something that is often missing in our day and age. However, this wasn't less true at the times of Socrates than it is today. How, then, does one arrive at such a self-knowledge? you wonder. This article aims precisely at answering this very question.

Again, the process to arrive at a self-understanding is a self-assessment. A self-assessment is an honest conversation with yourself about yourself. Often it will benefit you to include in that conversation other people who know and care about you. Such a process will lead to the discovery of things about yourself that you might have been aware of. If you want to make sure that you plan your career appropriately, it is particularly important for you to know the kind of person that you are. A career strategy needs not be too elaborate. How sophisticated and detailed you want to be is entirely up to you. However, a sound self-assessment will consider, among others, the following aspects of your life: your values, your passion, and your current knowledge. Let's now look at each one of these briefly.

- **Your Values**. Everyone has some things they consider more important than anything else in life. These are things they would likely always stand for no matter the circumstances. These things could be some social aspects of life (like family), some political convictions (like the right of women to vote), some religious beliefs, etc. Often, values are things for which someone would even consider dying. Nelson Mandela, for example, believed that apartheid was unjust and, in his own words, admitted that he was prepared to die to see that political system collapse. Whether they are conscious of them or not, everyone has values. You should know yours and take them into consideration when you plan your career and professional direction.

- **Your Passion.** We all have things that we are rather passionate about. These are things we enjoy. They are things we catch ourselves doing all the times. In a way, we are never tired of doing things we are passionate about. For example, some people enjoy reading. They read all the times and they do it effortlessly. Others enjoy public speaking. They find great joy and a huge sense of accomplishment when they are speaking to a live audience. Wherever they are, they quickly become the life of the party. People's passions also keep them awake at nights. If you pay attention to yourself, you will discover what your passions are. They are things about which you get very excited easily. When you are passionate about something, you always find a way to talk about it and you can do that all day. Your passions should be factored into your career plan.

- **Your Current Knowledge.** We all have some knowledge in certain particular areas. We may have acquired such knowledge from previous studies or personal experiences. Sometimes we forget that we have such knowledge because we take it for granted. It is, however, always good for you to think of all the assets (cognitive and others) you already have at your disposal. It does not matter how you got them. The most important thing is the fact that you do. As one bank puts it in a commercial, you may be richer than you think. Because of a lack of awareness of what we already have, sometimes we spend a lot of time, money and energy building new foundations when we should simply build on foundations we already have in place.

3. **Explore The Career Landscape.** Career research can take many forms from the general to the specific. It's normally better to gather more information than needed so you can analyze the data and then reject what you don't need.

Four areas come to mind to get you started:

A. Use information interviews to talk to others working in the proposed career field.

B. From the informational interviews learn what those working in the career read and study. How do they keep current? Build these activities into your career map planning.

C. If possible find an individual working in the planned field who can mentor you and help you assess your progress as you build and work your plan.

D. Keep abreast of industry trends. Go to conferences and trade shows, and use your networking abilities to add to your network. Have a list of career and industry blogs and websites that you regularly visit.

4. Flexibility will get you around roadblocks. With any career planning, one area most overlooked is financial planning. The two areas go hand in hand helping you reach your career objectives.

You must always plan for the worst possible financial situation.

You change careers and your income does not come up to previous levels for an extended period of time. You move to another more promising area and it takes longer than planned to find the right job. A promising career path hits an early dead-end. You work hard learning a new skill only to find the hard-earned technology is made obsolete with new software or the latest gizmo.

Your career plan must be realistic, with small positive steps taken over an extended period of time. Be sure your financial plan allows you the flexibility to continue on your career journey. As you uncover new career information, learn new skills and acquire added experience and abilities you will be in a better position to adjust your plan to overcome obstacles and roadblocks.

Career Planning Insurance:

We have insurance on almost everything. If you are holding an outdoor event you can even get insurance for the event if it rains.

So what about career planning insurance? No one that I'm aware of can sell you an insurance policy to protect your career. What you have to do is self-insured. That is you have to take responsibility for your own career.

Others are not going to make sure your career is moving forward and is becoming more valuable to you and to your employer. It is rarely productive to blame others for where you are or what you are doing. So it's up to you to ensure that your career is moving forward on the path that you planned.

We all know about the annual performance review. Yet there is a more important performance review than one done by your supervisor. Its the personal review you do on your own performance.

This review should be done at least every three months or sooner if you are just starting out in your career. First, update your resume. No need to rewrite the resume just add the appropriate information to the accomplishments, education and personal sections. If you have nothing to add to any of the sections it should tell you to start planning what you are going to do over the next three months.

After you've completed your performance review, take a close look at your work and your career. Do this analysis on a piece of paper. List what you like about your present job. Also, list what you don't like. Now ask yourself, "What can I do to do more of what I like?" And "What can I change about what I don't like?" From the answers to these two questions, you can add additional actions to your career plan.

Remember change is always difficult but if attempted in small steps you'll notice the improvements at your next planned performance review.

We are all living longer. Some long living retirees receive retirement benefits longer than the time that they worked to earn the pension. Social Security as we currently know it will be changed or it will go broke. All this means, in addition to your career plan, you need a well thought out financial plan.

You need to develop income coming in from a variety of sources. Multiple sources of income spread over a number of asset classes will also tend to reduce risk.

Of course, you must take advantage of the 401k offered by your employer. Roth IRA's or regular IRA's should be added to your financial plan. Opportunities to invest in real estate can also be considered. Everything starts with having a financial plan.

Second jobs can bring in extra income to invest. A neighbour works most Saturday nights as a bartender at a local country club. He earns more in tips and wages in six hours than he does working eight hours at his regular job. Another neighbour buys, fixes up and sells four to six cars a year. It has allowed him to buy real estate that provides him with additional income.

When you create additional sources of income you are adding career options that will be a benefit to you if you decide to change careers, retire early, or continue generating income when you do retire.

Moreover, your career plan will give you the flexibility to explore other careers or invest in a business and move to be self-employed. Career planning insurance means you take some of the risks out of your career.

CHAPTER SIX

Spiritual life planning and development

No building rises up without a plan. The higher and bigger the building the more extensive is the plan. No spiritual life shoots up to the heavens without a plan. There is a plan and this plan is called spiritual development plan. You may want to ask this question: What is my spiritual development plan?

It is a blueprint whereby a person knows how she is going to develop spiritually. In other words, it is a set of instructions whereby the person would know how she is going to proceed in her spiritual life until she reaches her goal in this area of her life.

Thus this plan is like the plan of a building. In the plan of a building we see the drawing of that building telling us where it stands, how deep is the foundation, the height of the building and the structures around the building. Seeing this drawing the engineers and the carpenters will be guided on how to put up the building.

In a spiritual development plan, we see the steps in the unfolding of this development of the spiritual life. We can notice the foundation of this life, the nature of this spiritual life and the environment around which it grows. Looking at this vision of the spiritual life the director or the life coach and the person building her spiritual life will be guided on what to do to progress in her spiritual life.

How To Assemble A Complete Spiritual Life

A strong spiritual house can't be built on one single cornerstone. We need, at minimum, four pillars for a good spiritual life, with every piece firmly anchored in truth and righteousness. Here the four essential pillars.

1. A Strong Spiritual Support System

To live a spiritual life, we need support. Many people associate spirituality with retreat and prayerful solitude, but as a general pattern, the avoidance of human relationships is spiritually unhealthy. Social experience represents a crucial part of spiritual development, for the following reasons:

Loving is a practice and responsibility, not merely an effect, of spiritual life. Heaven is no refuge for those who don't love on earth. The practice of love is not a mental exercise relative to a distant deity; love must be practised with real people. We advance spiritually as we exercise our capacity to consistently love and intimately serve fellow human beings.

Friendly feedback is divine course correction. Growth partners friends who support each other, and keep each other on track with good goals are indispensable to spiritual life. Life's greatest reflections and most valuable lessons come from people.

Intimacy can be not only challenging but also profoundly reassuring. Have you ever suffered a problem for a long time, only to find relief when you finally talked to somebody about it? God uses our friends to convey His "stamp of approval."

The energy of relationship kindles life and boosts awareness. Spiritual realization results from advances from one energy level to another. That's why the energy of interaction can accelerate personal transformation. It is a mysterious fact that when it comes to energy, one and one makes four. Each individual is but one pole of a cosmic battery whose potential is released only through interpersonal connections -- between you and your mate, you and your friends, or you and your world.

Here are three suggestions, starting small, for plugging into spiritual support in human relationships.

- **An Easy Warm-Up:** Have a weekly date with a good friend. It's easy to create interactions of questionable value, but for real support, do this: find at least one person who resonates with your higher spiritual values and make a regular date with that person.

- **Do Not Be Ashamed To Use Discrimination In Choosing The Influences In Your Life.** Sure, all human beings are equal in God but because people unfold at their own chosen speed, there are substantial differences between individuals. Just as God's lion is much stronger than God's mouse, one person may possess twice the spiritual power or intelligence of another. We all need inspiration as well as an opportunity to care for those who need our help. So put a lion a friend on your own level of development or higher on your social calendar. Regularly.

- **Good Exercise:** Move in with roommates, or join a church or other positively oriented organization. People who spend a significant amount of time relating enjoy much higher levels of energy. An individual's powers are magnified by the resonance of group energy. This principle applies equally to organizations and to living together in conscious roommate situations or intentional families.

Go for the gold! Move into a spiritual community. In a spiritually-oriented community, human interactions are elevated by mutually accepted principles of love and forgiveness.

2. Consistent Spiritual Practice With Clear Guidance

Spiritual seekers are fond of saying, "There are many paths up the mountain." But even if each path is complete and adequate in and of itself, progress along any of them requires steady effort. The best process in the world can't do you much good unless you do it and stick to it. Enlightenment requires commitment and consistency.

Investigating options for spiritual advancement can help a person piece together a useful big picture of spiritual life. However, a big picture of spiritual life is not the same as a spiritual life lived. Going to twenty car dealerships and coming home with eighty brochures about eighty different cars does not make you a car owner. Collecting the creeds from twenty religions does not make you a religious person -- much less a committed religious person.

It is rightly said that you cannot cross the river in more than one boat, for if you try to, you fall into the river. Therefore, spiritual life cannot succeed until you stop shopping and "buy" one method, one teacher, one path up the mountain.

The importance of a spiritual teacher. Westerners believe strongly in doing it themselves, and pride themselves in cutting out the spiritual middlemen. Some arguments for "going direct" may be valid, but people who resist human authorities also have problems with the highest Authority in the Universe! Sooner or later, if we want to get along with God, we will need to improve our relationship with authority.

Think of authorities as concentrated resources. We all can acknowledge that a person who knows a lot about something -- anything -- can be a useful resource for somebody who knows less and wants to know more. This is not a value judgment of any kind, just an observation of fact. It saves time and energy to go to a person in whom wisdom is densely concentrated.

Suggestions for consistent practice and clear guidance. Real commitment is the key to success in virtually any growth adventure. Here are three suggestions for applying commitment to your spiritual practice and guidance, no matter what level you buy in on.

- **An Easy Warm-Up:** Pick one book and study it in depth. Spiritual self-help and spiritual self-dabbling are different. When it comes to evolutionary progress, depth of experience beats breadth of exposure. You can get a lot more benefit from taking one self-help book and doing its entire process than from reading seventeen books without exploring any of them in depth.

- **Good Exercise:** Study with a group. Two heads are better than one -- and more heads are even better. It's truly dramatic how much smarter a group is that any of its members alone! Therefore, try to find an inspiring study group in the area of your spiritual interest -- and when you do, sign up, and stick to it.

Go for the gold! Find a real-life mentor. You probably have people in your life you can help because you have insights they don't have. Does that make you bad and wrong because to them, you are an authority? Of course not. And unless you think that you're at the very top of the evolutionary food chain, there's someone who can help you in a similar fashion. And maybe you need a mentor as much as your friends need you.

3. Spiritually Useful Purpose

Just working with our problems isn't enough. We must move beyond the level on which those problems exist, which is selfish living as a whole. That's where having a larger purpose in life becomes essential to spiritual progress. We escape suffering only by refocusing our energy on the highest possible purpose: to serve humanity, and further the divine purpose on this planet.

To transcend self-orientation doesn't require giving freely all the time. We can't just buy groceries and not ask our roommates to contribute; we can't just do work and not ask our clients or bosses to pay us. There has to be balanced in life. But there must be a place for selfless giving in everyone's life.

Suggestions for spiritually useful purpose. Your relationship to God, who is everywhere, is expressed as your relationship to all mankind.

Here are three everyday suggestions for relating to God through a spiritually useful purpose:

- **An Easy Warm-Up:** Lend a helping hand to a friend. You have plans to go to the beach, but your friend calls up to ask for help moving. You could say you already have other plans, but how good would that make her feel? How good would it make you feel? Everyone is obliged to transcend themselves in order to be happy. Help your friend happily, and go to the beach some other day.

- **Good Exercise:** Help the poor in spirit. You don't have to sell everything and join Mother Theresa's sisters in Calcutta to help the poor.

You can love the poor wherever you are. In America, poverty is much more common on the spiritual and emotional level than on the material. When you show compassion to a spiritually impoverished coworker or relative, you are certainly ministering to the poor.

Go for the gold! Support spiritual causes you believe in. You can serve the enlightenment of the human race by supporting a good spiritual cause or teaching. Find a way to serve -- volunteer work, financial support, etc. -- that suits your temperament and resources. It doesn't matter what you do as long as you do something. Any person who works in any way to support a good spiritual cause extends the good work.

4. Right Livelihood

Work will always remain an essential part of spiritual life. What better way to serve our fellows and transcend our egos than by surrendering ourselves to creative effort?

People get confused about right livelihood. It's not so much what you do as how you do it. One of the greatest joys in life is the joy of work consciously performed for a good purpose -- with the intention of blessing those who will benefit from it. Any work is consecrated if it is dedicated to a sacred purpose, such as the service of man or the love of God.

Wherever we find ourselves, our actions can be viewed from the true, eternal, spiritual perspective. Heavenly standards for appropriate living reflect the essential and eternal realities of God and Good. In that sense, the standards for right livelihood or for good job performance will never change, and there's No part or position that's any further "off the path" than any other.

The evaluation of success is based on how well spiritual challenges are handled. A person can succeed admirably in spiritual terms, yet never get rich. But here are good news for all spiritual seekers: Some worldly standards are spiritual values as well -- for example, character-building virtues like flexibility, cooperativeness, calm in the face of adversity, goodwill towards others, diligence, and honesty. Any individual with these "qualifications" will make valuable contributions -- on the material as well as on the spiritual level -- to any task.

Here are suggestions for turning your job, whatever it is, into a spiritual venture.

- **An Easy Warm-Up:** Economic self-responsibility. The most basic, but most important spiritual challenge of work is to cheerfully and responsibly embrace your obligation to support yourself and others who may depend on you.
- **Good Exercise:** Spiritualize the routine moments. Whenever you feel that your circumstances and activities do not spiritually inspire you, you are probably ignoring the real spiritual challenge at hand. For example, a spiritual response to a boring job is to transcend your negative reactions to circumstances and bring real life and energy to your work. By exercising your spiritual muscles in routine or mundane circumstances, you will improve yourself and your work environment at the same time.

Go for the gold! Rise to a difficult occasion. Spiritualize your livelihood by bringing your spiritual values to the more difficult moments of life. For example, you can apply the spiritual values of patience and goodwill to score a spiritual victory with a customer or a co-worker who is being obnoxious. By committing yourself to rise above such difficulties you can make it a real stretch to go to work each day.

Most Important Steps To Take On "Spiritual Life" With "Work Balance

In life one comes to a point after a series of breakdowns where he finds himself inadequate. He is just not able to think anything other than finding food and paying bills. He loses it when it comes to a better quality of life and he finds himself lacking and envying those who have the liberty and time to pursue a nice joyous moment. He is down in the dumps bound by the bondage of desolation and feels enslaved in mediocrity. If you feeling dejected and nothing is working out, its time for a reality check and reorganize your strategy towards current life. It is wise to take stock from time to time and keep these first three points towards getting yourself up and ready for a better and successful life.

1. **Recognize The Futility Of The Current Approach And Desire To Find Out Why?**

Life provides enough latitude for realizing this predicament. It is rather urgent in some case or sooner or later in others. It is for those who are troubled who take the first step to find out if their approach is flawed in any way. If their approach is rational in all ways and even then, the results are not as expected then there is surely a problem that needs to be addressed. This futility generates an immense desire (Sub-Iccha) the primordial desire to find out what is on the flip side of the normal known approach. If you have already gotten this feeling, you have successfully passed on the next step.

2. **Find Out The Root Cause Of Dissatisfaction:**

Once the futility of the current approach is established and you are convinced with the flaw, you would need to find out the root cause of the problem. Is it that you are aware of the something that you are neglecting? Is it that you are impervious to your soul cry? Is it that you are ignoring the most important value that you have inbuilt in your system? Most likely "Yes", If you have a feeling that you were obsessed with the idea that your family and social standing was more important than your innermost passion in life then you are heading in the direction of finding out the root cause of your dissatisfaction.

Identify that which is most appealing and that you have been neglecting so far. Feel the reason why you have been neglecting this. Is it because your passion does not generate income? Or do you feel, there will be no purchase from society?

Is it that you are ashamed that what if your idea fails and you are not sure that you can shoulder the responsibility. So once you have given the thought to identify the root and found the reason for neglect, you could write down the reasons for not pursuing those items in the list.

3. Where Do You Want To Go From Here?

Once you have identified that your approach towards life and that it has been severely derailed from the high road of freedom, then it's time to pause and reset. You also identified different reasons that contributed to the failure and non-pursuit of your passions. The next step is to find out where the dissatisfaction is residing. Is it because of the mind or the heart? The contributors of dissatisfaction can be of many categories, there could be materially related such as money, fame or education, or mental peace. In any case, identify the role of, your mind and it's cause for desire and control. You will be surprised to note that the lack of pursuit in the direction of your own spirit causes the discomfort and stress amongst the constant chatter of the mind.

4. Enquire About The Fact Of "Who You Really Are"? Are You The Mind?

If you have identified that the mind is the main impediment in your journey of life then zero in on that. The best way is to contemplate in the actions of your mind. It's easy to plot a pattern yourself on the travails of the futile attempts of the mind in the matters that you have no control. Start observing the mind from a distance by dissociating with it for some time. Then you would see the futility of some of its actions, specifically in the matters of no control. Events and people's reactions, attitudes etc. Organize the pattern of these recognitions that you have made from this distance. Once you are observing the mind the mind loses it momentum and begins to falter and slows down. This place of observance is the place of peace and tranquillity and that's the "true self". Feel that and stay there. It gives great joy to be able to see your mind looking back for your support and know you are not behind it. Then you would be entering into the door of freedom.

Freedom from slavery, freedom from the bondage and misrepresented deceit from the mind. You will also know who is the boss? In this entity that you living in. You know your mind is related to the body and then begin steps to go to the next stage of managing the mind by allowing, and not controlling. The pointer here is to allow yourself to observe and not control from a distance. This very state of observance is most widely known as "Meditation". In this inquiry, you will clearly know that you are not your mind as you thought you were. You are also will know that your approach was flawed, you will also know that you have been living in a false utopia managed by a deceiving mind representing reality as it sees from a bifocal lens. Once you know this you are ready to take on the next step.

5. To Perfect Staying In The Zone And Balance Work Commitments

From step 4 you have reached a state of recognizing your mind and recognizing yourself. You have also tasted the peace and joy of "the self". You have also experienced the unlimited divine wisdom of staying in the zone and not side with the mind. You now are able to get the point that thoughts have a non-sense value and contribute to mental and physical stress. You start preparing to stay in the zone of observance and watch. Slowly and steadily you start thinking out of the box of limitedness and begin to realize the benefits of being in "Self". If "The self " is real and unchanging every time you visit the zone, then you know that you arrived "at home" the real place of being. This real place is the incentive to go back every time just to be there. You start to meditate many times during the day and the repetitions become more frequent. You will start gaining the wisdom of the unknown and start releasing the wisdom of the known mind. Vedantha or "Ved" "knowledge" and "Anthaha" meaning "The End" is the true meaning of Vedantha.

So you will be in a position to grasp and translate the immense infinite possibilities by just dropping your past beliefs and doctrines from the one-sided mind. You will stop thinking of identifying yourself with the mind as the be all and end all of all things and start looking at the mind as a tool to discharge your worldly affairs. The mind at this stage becomes submissive to your call and command and you would begin to use it as a tool. This mind surprisingly becomes subservient to the self upon realization. It is the greatest tool that you can ever possess and also the greatest demon that you faced in your life. What this realization brings about is a change turning the tables of your destiny in life. Perspectives change, and a renewed born again into the spirit feeling is reached.

Most people often have the question that in a spiritual world that worldly matters are put on the shelf. I would rather say that worldly matters are injected with a divine wisdom that surpasses all understanding. Work, bills, commitments as you saw earlier are not ties to a limited provision as you before. You begin to see a provision in every action you take from the self. Your sincerity increases with integrity and thankfulness for the current job you have. You would be grateful for a million things including simple things like the ability to wake up in the morning and having good health. You begin to see the world full of opportunities and your responsibility in this world is provided by the universe. Your work is layered on top of the self and then your mind executes the command from the place of actual reality. It becomes as simple as that.

Ways To Lead A More Spiritual Life

Spirituality is not a boxed and packaged concept that requires an "all in" commitment. It is not an all or nothing proposition. And it's not about a label. Living a more spiritual life can mean finding the meaning beyond the ordinary in everything we do. It can mean aligning with our true purpose so that we find joy in every step. It can mean letting go of the negative minds that hold us back.

It's not complicated. But it is revolutionary. It is a powerful way to transform your everyday life as you continue to go to work, care for your family, and hang out with your friends. Here are five ways you can lead a more spiritual life every day.

1. Breathe

Easy, right? We're doing it anyway. All the time. So we're halfway there. Now, what happens if you turn your attention to that breath? When we turn our attention to our breath and focus it as single-pointedly as possible, the benefits that come from that simple action are huge. We can use this practice to:

- Let go of anger, stress and frustration: a few moments of breath can prevent us from snapping at our partner or getting ourselves into hot water at work

- Access the calm inside the storm: as the world spins out of control around us, we can prevent ourselves from getting swept up in its currents by simply breathing and focusing on the rock-solid strength that can be found within
- Find our inner wisdom: instead of making (often disastrous) decisions from a place of fear or frustration, we can take a few minutes to breathe and find a more reliable place from which to make decisions that move us forward instead of keeping us stuck

2. Give

We don't have to have to give celebrity-sized donations to make a difference in the world. If you have the means, making monetary donations is a wonderful way to give. But it is not the only way. The simplest acts of giving can spread happiness like wildfire. Both within your own mind and the minds of others. We can give a small amount of time and effort and reap big rewards. You can change someone's day, and maybe even their entire life, with the tiniest act of giving such as:

- Holding a door open

- Letting someone in your lane in heavy traffic (no matter how late you are)

- Telling a friend you are thinking about them (even if it's just a simple text message)

3. Pay Attention

It's so easy to get wrapped up in our own stories. We live at a frenetic pace. Our days are filled with endless lists of things that we need to do, and in order to get them done we often enter a head down, blinders on, full-speed ahead mode of existing. The people around us are no longer individuals but faceless blurs, and maybe even obstacles. We lose our connection to others.

On a larger scale, a lost connection with others is at the root of world conflict. The simple mental acknowledgement that others are important and deserve to be happy is at the root of world peace. Your mission is quite simple:

- Look at one person a day. Really look at them. But not in a creepy, staring way that might freak them out

- Think about what they may have gone through that day. Are they having a good day? A bad day? Are they fighting with their partner? Are they missing somebody? Did they just achieve something great?

- Hold the simple thought "You are important. Your happiness is important."

- Get on with your busy day

4. Be Quiet

Quiet is something of which we are often unconsciously afraid. Why? It is the great revealer. It pulls back the curtains of our mind and shows us what's going on in there. And it ain't always pretty. There's a lot of noise in there. A lot of unresolved hurts. A dash of anger. A pinch of fear. Mixed in with some anxiety and a whole lot of meaningless chatter about our grocery list and whether or not we need to change the oil in our car.

So go easy on yourself. Start with just five minutes a day. Turn off the television. Turn off the radio. Silence the cell phone. Tear yourself away from the computer or any other devices that are calling your name.

And get quiet. See what your mind is really up to. Because what our mind is up to is what drives us, whether we are conscious of it or not. We could be letting those fears, anxieties, and old hurts that are lurking in there making decisions for us NOW. Although it may be uncomfortable at first, looking at our mind fully gives us back conscious control over everything that we think, say, and do.

5. Smile

Historically, this is the piece of advice that annoyed me more than anything else. The angry-young-woman version of myself wanted to give someone a smack upside the head every time they said that to me. But in my (not so) wise and (not so) old age, I'm ready to admit that the advice was sound. For several reasons:

- Smiles are like puppies' and kittens and babies. People feel good when they see them. And maybe then they smile. And someone else sees it. And they smile. And... you get the idea.

- The physical action of smiling reminds your mind to be happy. No matter what happens. Our ability to be happy under even the most difficult of circumstances is stronger than we may think. A simple smile can remind us of that. When our face is smiling, our mind often follows suit.

- A smile is a world shaper. We all want to experience more happiness in our lives. If we want that experience, we need to create it. The smile has a magical ability to shape that experience for us, in its ability to lighten the minds of both ourself and others.

Spirituality is not limited to any one way of thinking or doing. We can each feel inspired to find our own spirituality in our own way, and stay connected to it so that we can experience the true meaning in our lives. And most importantly, we can enjoy the journey.

CHAPTER SEVEN

Entrepreneurship skills for lifetime sustainability

The state of being an entrepreneur can be realized when one engages in profitable risks and creates something of value. Entrepreneurs are defined by their habit of innovating and redefining market trends and limits. Regardless of their heredity, their background, their exposures and what not; entrepreneurs are people who are able to develop new businesses and affect the overall condition of the global economy. Given this, it is obvious that being an entrepreneur is no joke. Aside from the stress of creating and running a business, the additional responsibility of being able to contribute something significant to society is given to them.

Talent is no longer enough in today's highly competitive marketplace, so one needs to develop his or talent into a skill. A skill is a way of doing something in a way that is unique, and unusual, and that separates one from others. Being an entrepreneur is not enough, one has to develop entrepreneurial skills, and I will be sharing some of them with you,

1. Risk Taking

Before embarking on the journey of entrepreneurship, one has to be prepared for the risk that has to be taken especially when one is just starting. When I started my own journey, though I have gotten to the height I had loved to attain, I risked my time, my education, my resources my finance, and even my health at some point. The journey is filled with a lot of uncertainty, and oftentimes, it looks like jumping into the unknown and hoping that one will, over time learn the ropes and get by.

Since risk-taking is inevitable, then there is need for a risk management system. That is, how do you take calculated risks? And that's where planning and organisation come into play. Before taking risk, I think one needs to read in between the lines, and if possible, come up with a plan B in case things don't go as planned, as they sometimes will, so that you don't get your fingers burnt.

2. Persistence

I have observed that entrepreneurs are not the brightest, sharpest, or most intelligent people, those are the attributes of scholars, and academics, not entrepreneurs. One denominator of entrepreneurs is that they are persistent. They may not have all the degrees, but they know what they want and they won't stop until they get it.

Given that less than forty per cent of businesses today, survive past five years, then only the "die-hard," strong headed people who are so stubborn that fly in the sky, to make their dreams come true. In the absence of wings, they will run, and when they can't run, they will crawl. By every means possible, they want to survive past their struggles, until they achieve success. That's the entrepreneur's spirit, or what some people call the warrior spirit. Warriors don't get tired until they win. "It's a tough world out there! mediocre can't survive for too long and when they do, they can only operate as peripheral players."

3. Capital

An entrepreneur has got to be money wise. Though the reason he/she is in business is not just to make profit, money serves as the grease that keeps the wheel of the business moving, smoothly. It is always good practice to have an emergency fund solely for the business outfit, and the fund will be useful when, perhaps, when one to seize a business opportunity.

Money management also has effect on employee's salary. If the entrepreneur is not money wise, sooner or later, he/she will be owing to his/her accountant or secretary three month's salary. Money is also needed in implementing the growth strategy.

Aside from financial capital, entrepreneurs need human capital. You cannot succeed alone, so you need like-minded people, people who share the same vision with you. Grooming and helping others to discover and develop their potentials is the work of the business leader.

Presently, we have the 7th generation of Henry Ford championing the course of the Ford Group of Companies. Until you have developed people, your business does not have a life of its own. The latter means that when you are sick, the business is sick. When you are financially down, the business is financially down, and perhaps when you die, the business dies. As entrepreneurs, we have to create the big picture for others to see.

A vision compelling enough to motivate your team so that when we eventually die, the business empire outlives us.

Lastly, entrepreneurs need to develop relational capital. As your business expands, you can easily become isolated from some of your workers, which is not supposed to happen. Charles Schwab, a very successful entrepreneur, once decided to travel in a train, instead of travelling in an aeroplane, to enable him to discuss with his driver. Don't forget that the higher you go in management (or any business for that matter), the less of technical skill you need, and you need more of people skills.

4. Network

A network could simply be a friendship founded on business for the mutual benefit of one another. Your network consists of those people whose contact you have and had developed friendship with. The truth is that every new positive friendship we develop, based on business, can be of great benefits, not just today alone, but sometime in the distant future. Furthermore, someone's call on your behalf, or his/her handwritten letter, or better still, his/her business card can take your business to the next level. It can open doors for you.

Your network should also consist of people who have the same vision, passion, and motivation as you. It should consist of people with whom you can have monthly or bi-monthly meetings, where you sharpen each other's axes. It has been said that you are just three persons away from whatever you want in life.

5. Innovation

An entrepreneur is an innovator, who paints a big picture that motivates a marching order. The entrepreneur must be willing to always re-invent himself/herself, at all times, to remain relevant in the marketplace. Since the particular needs of customers change per time, entrepreneurs must embrace change. "If the rate of change outside your organisation is greater than the rate of change inside your organisation, then the end is not in sight.

Habits Of Highly Effective Entrepreneurs

Why is adequacy fundamental for progress? Since, in every single basic leadership process, adequacy assumes a focal part. Adequacy comes down to delivering wanted outcomes. The best business visionaries have aced adequacy since it influences them to work more 🗆uick-witted, taking out superfluous exertion and sat idle. Achievement can't occur with any consistency when drawn nearer in an apathetic, erratic, hit-or-miss form. The best business people don't engage straightforwardness or complication as a piece of their basic leadership process. They make a point to be itemized, sorted out and completely arranged before executing on any objective or plan. To take after are eight propensities profoundly successful business visionaries practice to remain in the stream of positive development.

1. Visionary

The most persuasive business visionaries invest a lot of energy in their heads considering and visioning. They are normally creative and need being in the steady procedure of revelation. They acknowledge their creative energy as their most capable resource. They have dependably hoped against hope, and to transform those fantasies into a reality. This visionary ⬚uality separates them from other people who don't hope against hope as large or as immense. The individuals who emerge from the pack see no end-date to their innovativeness, their prosperity, their capacity to profit, include themselves in new pursuits, and to do what they trust they can even now imagine and accomplish. They are not a one-and-done sort of persona.

2. Morning People

Compelling business people rise early trusting in the idea of; the brisk riser gets the worm. They begin every day with some type of physical movement. It's simply the techni⬚ue they use to wake up, get their blood pumping and their mind sharp. They want to get into the workplace before others to work without intrusion on the objectives they set for themselves the prior night. Stretching out beyond the amusement and one stage in front of their pressure. At the point when the earth is tran⬚uil and free of diversions they achieve their work all the more productively and with higher quality.

Getting in early additionally liberates time up for them to be completely present in aiding and working together with partners once they touch base in the workplace.

3. Planned

Fruitful business people increment their productivity by putting work first and mingling second. Mingling is critical and nurturing for them. They see the incentive in persuading out to associate with individuals, not only for the human cooperation and sentiments of interconnectedness but since being around others lessens pressure and builds advancement. They plan this time toward the day's end when their work-weights are off. This enables them to be completely present to those they are associating and creating associations with. Since they sort out their lives like this, it ensures they will work proficiently in any condition they put themselves in.

4. Rest

Fruitful business visionary's never underestimate the significance of rest. They want to be sharp, candidly accessible, and on-the-ball in every aspect of their profession. There is a demonstrated and all around recorded collection of proof on the bi-directional connection amongst rest and stress: an absence of rest makes expansion in enthusiastic reactivity and declines in dissatisfaction resilience, which add to one more night of poor rest. It's a terrible cycle. Active business visionaries would prefer not to sit idly being up during the evening worrying about how inadequately or insufficiently they took care of circumstances or individuals amid the day. On the off chance that poor resting designs are left unmanaged, adequacy winds up inconceivable. Effective business visionaries assume that work isn't going anyplace. They cut out the fundamental time for rest and are all the better for it. Since they regard their rest and make a point to get enough of it, they make themselves less inclined to succumb to sentiments of burnout, falling prey to lost profitability, expanded medical problems and missed days of work.

5. Straightforwardness

Straightforwardness is the mystery weapon successful business visionaries swear by. They're known to make and live about fanatically by basic yet down to earth schedules.

Making basic schedules causes them to abstain from going up against workloads which are past what they can sensibly handle. Fruitful business people are the most beneficial in accomplishing their coveted outcomes when they aren't overpowered by pressure.

Thus, they set points of confinement around themselves. They stress less over satisfying others and more about creating brilliant work. The points of confinement they put for their advantage give them a feeling of organization over their lives, their workload, and in having the capacity to execute as adequately and effectively as would be prudent.

6. Diary

One of the most effortless approaches to expand adequacy is to influence it to propensity to write in a diary. Effective business people put pen-to-paper and record all that is critical to them. They compose records, objectives, or compose to vent their disappointments. Composing has demonstrated to have various advantages. It requires commitment from the two sides of the cerebrum, making the conceptualizing or critical thinking process more total and creative. Further, composition is urgent with regards to settling enthusiastic reactivity. It loosens up feelings caused by pressure or struggle by giving a genuinely necessary detach from the monotonous routine of reliable talking, messaging, accepting calls, and different diversions which come along with electronic gadgets. Exceptionally viable businesspeople esteem the way toward composing since it places them in contact with the more existential parts of life, helping them to remember the master plan of what they're taking a stab at.

7. Adaptable

As critical as standard may be, the best business visionaries comprehend it is basic they be sufficiently adaptable to rotate on request in light of unanticipated or evolving conditions. Being sufficiently adaptable to alter course extraordinarily builds their odds at progress, and it additionally improves their particular learning, development, and training. The schedules they live by are basic by plan since this effortlessness is anything but difficult to keep up regardless of their conditions. Effective business people make it a propensity to just need the minimum necessities. This expands efficiency because their set-up to work and convey doesn't require anything uncommon for them to be successful whether they're at the shoreline or in the workplace.

8. Inquisitive

Fatigue is the enemy of viability; which is the reason the best business people are never exhausted. They joyfully spend unlimited hours working and doing what they want to do. They make it a propensity to be open and inquisitive about everything. This interest keeps them making inquiries and creating thoughts for what they're subsequent stages will be. Since they stay open and inquisitive, it is difficult to deplete their innovative stores. They generally have some little thought they are anxious to investigate at a later time. Interest is simply one more perspective which contributes their adequacy and achievement. Interest is the contrast between normal achievement and incredible triumphs. Normal individuals tend to quit working when they come up short on innovative vitality, while exceedingly successful business visionaries have a drastically extraordinary approach in that they generate constantly new thoughts or ways to take after.

9. Personal Branding

Is there such a thing as brand loyalty? Of Course.... some people prefer Coke, while others drink Pepsi. That's an obvious comparison. How about brand loyalty in cars, or the restaurants that you eat at? Again, easy to see, but what is often overlooked is that individual people have a brand too. Who you are and what you offer makes all the difference in the world when it comes to building your business... that's right, your personal brand is more important than your organizational brand. What's interesting is that for entrepreneurs, most of the time your personal branding shapes your organization's brand and culture.

As you establish your business and you start interacting with other folks, your customers and clients- you will be known for something. Unfortunately, for those who don't think about this point, sometimes that is a negative thing. The point here is that you want to control what you are known for.

This isn't as complex as it sounds. The most important part is deciding- what is it that you want to be known for? Great communications, great service, great... you fill in the blank. After you decide what that it is, then you must make sure your values and your goals take your brand into consideration. Finally, the hardest part is this: Your Actions and Activities must always support your brand image. That's it. And it's probably one of the most important things you must establish to grow your business successfully.

Easy Steps to Develop Your Entrepreneurship Skills

So, how to go about this entrepreneurship skills development path and what are the steps to follow? Here are some:

- **Learning To Look At The Big Picture**

Entrepreneurship skills development starts with you seeing the bigger picture. What this implies that you have to understand the industry that you are in, and how different domains are interconnected. It means having an insight into how companies operate on a fundamental level and how businesses are built from the ground up. If you are someone who is not willing to keep himself updated with the market trends, then there is not much potential for success. Neither for you nor for your organization.

- **An Appetite For Success**

Entrepreneurship skills development is as much about learning and acquiring new skills as it is about having an appetite for success. You have to have the will to make things happen, and this requires not only motivation but an ability to push yourself beyond what's required of you. Understand this, this is your company that you are working to build and nobody is going to care about it apart from you. Be hungry to get more accomplished. You can get to this by ensuring that you plan your day well in advance. Remember, failing to plan is planning to fail!

- **Valor**

Don't sulk if you feel you don't self-confidence, at least in any meaningful amount. The fact of the matter is this, very few of us, yes, even your idols had much self-confidence when they started out. The only reason you don't have confidence is that you haven't experienced much successes or failures. Only through experience, you going to develop any confidence. Have the guts to act like you do. Make people believe in you. That's enough to make those investors trust you and give your venture a shot. Entrepreneurship skills development can re⊠uire you to fake confidence at times, go for it. Nobody has it when they start out.

- **Decisiveness**

If you ask different people regarding decisiveness, then you will probably get a number of different answers. For the most part, all you will get is fuzzy notions about decisiveness and leadership. Decisiveness will play a big role on your path towards Entrepreneurship skills development.

Steps To Creating An Entrepreneur Mindset

There are a lot of people who want to be an entrepreneur and acquire the wealth that can come with being one. However, most people have no definite plan or path to achieving this desire. A critical shift must happen in order to reach your goal of being a successful entrepreneur. The shift is in creating an entrepreneur mindset. It occurs when the following steps happen.

- **Find Your Purpose**

You will need to find a service, product or idea that you are passionate about and turn it into a business. Without a purpose, desire or passion you will get nowhere. It will need to be a strong enough desire to withstand any obstacle you encounter. Your purpose will require you to form a new outlook. A new outlook that requires strength and creativity. It will require you to always look for the opportunity from any failure. If your desire is strong enough you will make your business successful no matter how many failures you encounter. Some of the most successful people in life, such as Thomas Edison, encountered thousands of failures before being successful. His desire and purpose were so strong that he continued when others would have quit.

- **Organized Plan**

Once you have a concept, purpose and a definite desire to pursue your business, you'll need to figure out how you're going to get there. Be specific about what your goals are and the steps that will need to be taken to achieve them. Without a specific and organized plan with dates assigned to when goals and tasks will be met, you will flounder. You will need to be accountable to yourself, your mentors and those who are involved in your business.

- **Create Action**

If you do not take action you will not have a business. It seems obvious that you would need action in order to build a business however, most people fail to take action.

People find reasons to procrastinate, but people who have a burning desire to succeed will take action no matter what is put in their path. Break your plan into small daily steps that you accomplish every day to start the momentum and then build on it.

- **Surround Yourself with People who will Encourage You**

There will inevitably be days where there are problems and setbacks and you will need to be around those people who encourage you when it gets tough. There will inevitably be well-meaning friends and family that will be discouraging and you can easily find yourself falling into bad habits which will cause you to fail. You will need to gain the strength to ignore them and form friendships and alliances with those that are constructive, positive and helpful.

- **Create Positive Habits**

You need to create positive habits that take you closer to your goals. Part of that includes surrounding yourself with successful entrepreneurs and learning what successful habits they formed. It also involves acquiring knowledge through books in your chosen field. It also requires reading books about how highly successful people achieved their success and implementing those methods into your routine. One of the most successful businessmen in the world, Bill Gates, spends a day out of the week reading and acquiring knowledge.

Review your Purpose Daily

Always remind yourself why you're pursuing your business. Reviewing your why will help strengthen your resolve. Spending time first thing in the morning and in the evening before bed and reviewing your purpose helps to push you further.

Creating an entrepreneurial mindset is critical to your success. Becoming an entrepreneur is no easy task, however, it is one of the most rewarding experiences you can have. Knowing that you can build a business and wealth no matter what you encounter in life is an amazing experience. Devote your time to developing a new and positive mindset and experience how far you will go.

Developing a New Self-Perception for better Tomorrow

You know what's good about life? We can look at each day as a clean slate. We start off fresh, with no mistakes and nothing to regret. If we choose we can use the day to create positive experiences and fulfil our dreams.

That doesn't always happen, however. Sometimes life gets away from us and we get caught up in drama and turmoil. We tend to the needs of those around us and put ourselves last. It can be shocking to realize how completely we drown ourselves in minutiae instead of thinking about the big picture and our own happiness.

Many people find it easy to constantly put our children, spouse, friends and career ahead of ourselves. In our society, that type of behaviour is rewarded. Yet, it isn't always satisfying and can leave one feeling lost or unfulfilled. Often people don't give themselves a timeout. They don't place enough emphasis on introspection, which makes the problems they have and the sadness they feel, continue

Fortunately, it's never too late to take a look within ourselves. Think about what makes us happy and explore things that interest us. You may want to make a list of what is important to you and of things you've always wanted to do. Here are a few ideas to get you started.

Write down what you want out of life. Is it a different career? What books would you like to read? Where would you like to travel? Have you always wanted a child? What about travel or hobbies? Some people dream about starting their own business. Ask yourself if that could be you.

Get started right away. It's your life, you may as well begin realizing what it could be. Ask yourself, what is important to you as human being? What are your hopes and goals? How do you feel about yourself? Who would you be if you could start over in life?

There's virtually no wrong answer to these questions. Be honest with yourself and decide what changes you want to make with your life. Prioritize your list and decide which are immediate and which are long-term changes or goals. It's important to realize which will change your life for the better and which are desirable but not absolutely necessary to make you happy.

Ways to Begin to Change Your Perspective of Everyday Life

Here are a few ways to begin to change your perspective on everyday life. Please be intelligent about safety when practising any of them:

1. **Cover One Eye And Carefully Explore The Spaces Around You:** Just losing your normal 3-dimensional way of seeing is enough to make some people dizzy. That might suggest a very limited 'view' of the visual world. Break the habit of believing the viewable world is always the same. What is real to you often depends on how you see it. Unless you are conscious of your own ability to interpret your senses, you will be trapped in the one that gets to you first.

2. **Take Something That Bothers You A Lot, And Defend It Adamantly:** This isn't giving in to someone else's opinion. This is to practice your ability to

decide for yourself what your opinions are. Granted, this is not an easy exercise, but it will open you up completely to being tolerant of the opinions of others. By example, you will be able to show that differences in opinion can lead to twice the chance to learn.

3. **Imagine Looking Through The Eyes Of Your Baby/Pet:** This is like covering one eye. Most people are visual enough to make this a pretty easy exercise. The trick is to stay in the 'bay view' as long as you can. A few seconds is interesting, but a few minutes could give you a completely new idea of the attitudes behind your surrogate pair of eyes.

4. **When Looking At Something Really Big, Examine A Very Small Part Of It; Look For Any Re-Occurring Patterns:** A wise man once said, 'regardless of scale, nature repeats itself.' This axiom can be found in so many instances throughout life, it's quite astounding. And once you see the connection between the very big and the very small, you can begin to see that there might very well be connections throughout nature, and therefore life.

5. **Blindfold Yourself In A Public Place.** (Please, assistance required!): This one is obvious. You want to try depending on your other senses to do what you would normally take for granted. Not enough? Throw on a pair of earphones to simulate difficulty or inability to hear and experience your attempts to receive a perception of your surroundings.

6. **Imagine Being An Alien From Another Planet, Here To Understand Human Behavioural Patterns:** If you try to disassociate from the human race, and stop trying to take everyday typical patterns for granted, and ask why do they do that, you might begin to notice a lot of interesting things about us! Obviously, I'm not suggesting that you become effectively anti-social. Remember, this is only an exercise in changing your perspective.

CONCLUSION

We live our lives on a daily basis. We have our routines, our obligations and our enjoyments. How much of your daily actions are creating a better life for you tomorrow? Everyone ultimately wants a better life; it's whether or not they want to put in the effort. In all aspects of life, what we do today, builds our tomorrow and beyond.

One of my favourite personal quotes goes as follows: "Is what you are doing today, creating a better life for you?" On a daily basis, our actions, no matter how minimal they may seem, have an effect on our future. Everything from money handling, exercise, diet, who we talk to and what we buy, among other things, help decide the type of future we will have. There are many things we just can't control, but also, there is much that we can. How our lives turn out is ultimately up to us. If we decide to put a certain amount of money in an investment account, rather than on items we don't need, our financial situation will be different. If we eat fast food, it often has an effect on our overall energy and demeanour, and this can also change our work ethic and how our future turns out. It is just amazing how even the littlest things can significantly affect our lives.

Imagine this: you decide to go to an educational luncheon and strike up a conversation with someone who has connections to various job opportunities that you would really enjoy. Things would be vastly different if you decided to stay home and watch some TV because you were just too tired to go. When opportunities arise, take them seriously, no matter how small, as they can completely alter your life for the better. Maybe one night you decided to read a motivational book instead of doing nothing and it inspired you to do something great. You may decide to go on a random hiking trip one day, and love it so much, that you make it a regular part of your routine. This can have a profound effect on your health.

It is incredible how even the smallest decisions we make on a daily basis can change our future. The decisions you make and actions you take on a daily basis should be taken seriously because you never know how they can affect your tomorrow. Make what you are doing today create a better tomorrow. It is a constant, daily process to create that better life. Think about your actions and continue to make the right decisions for yourself.

Good luck!

www.ingramcontent.com/pod-product-compliance
Lightning Source LLC
Chambersburg PA
CBHW072014230526
45468CB00021B/1463